Published by
Cazu Productions and Publishing
mail@alcazu.com

ISBN-13: 978-1523781997
ISBN-10: 1523781998

Introduction

The Moorlands of England's Southwest corner provides us with
the most wondrous landscapes.

My own first visit to this rocky terrain was many years ago. I have
always known that there exists a magical beauty here. I have made
many visits to these lands but I never really did fully connect with
nor understand that elusive magic, so I therefor embarked on this
study and investigation. It has resulted by way of this collection of
drawings, paintings, and book. fortunatly I also found something
of what I was searching for..

These pages are arranged at random and do not in anyway represent
a linear route across the moors. Some images derive from Dartmoor
and others from Bodmin Moor. Neither do the image titles indicate
their locations. This is your challenge. If you can identify nine of the
specific locations that are illustrated within this book and answer the
question 'What is a Tor?' Please e-mail: mail@alcazu.com The first
correct set of answers will be rewarded with an original signed work
of art. The following nine correct replies will receive a high
quality signed print.

I very much hope that you like and enjoy this book.

Al Cazu

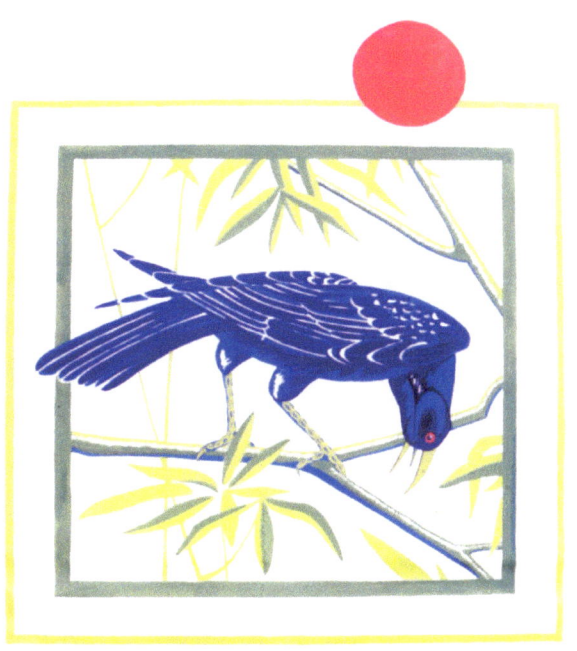

Red Sun & Crow
Linocut Print 300 x 300 mm

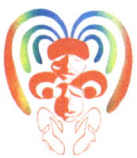

Winter Sky
Pencil 297 x 210 mm

In wintertime the weather here
is often harsh and at times it can
be positively wicked. When the
ground freezes and snow falls
it is difficult to believe that any
form of life can survive here
during the winter months. On
some days even the sky becomes
so hostile that surly no bird
would ever consider venturing
from the nest.

Moorland Snow
Pencil 300 x 500 mm

These lands are not easy to navigate at anytime. Without the Tors that provide such prominent landmarks and waypoints, path finding would be near impossible. When snow blankets the entire landscape these petrified giants remain steadfast and signpost the way.

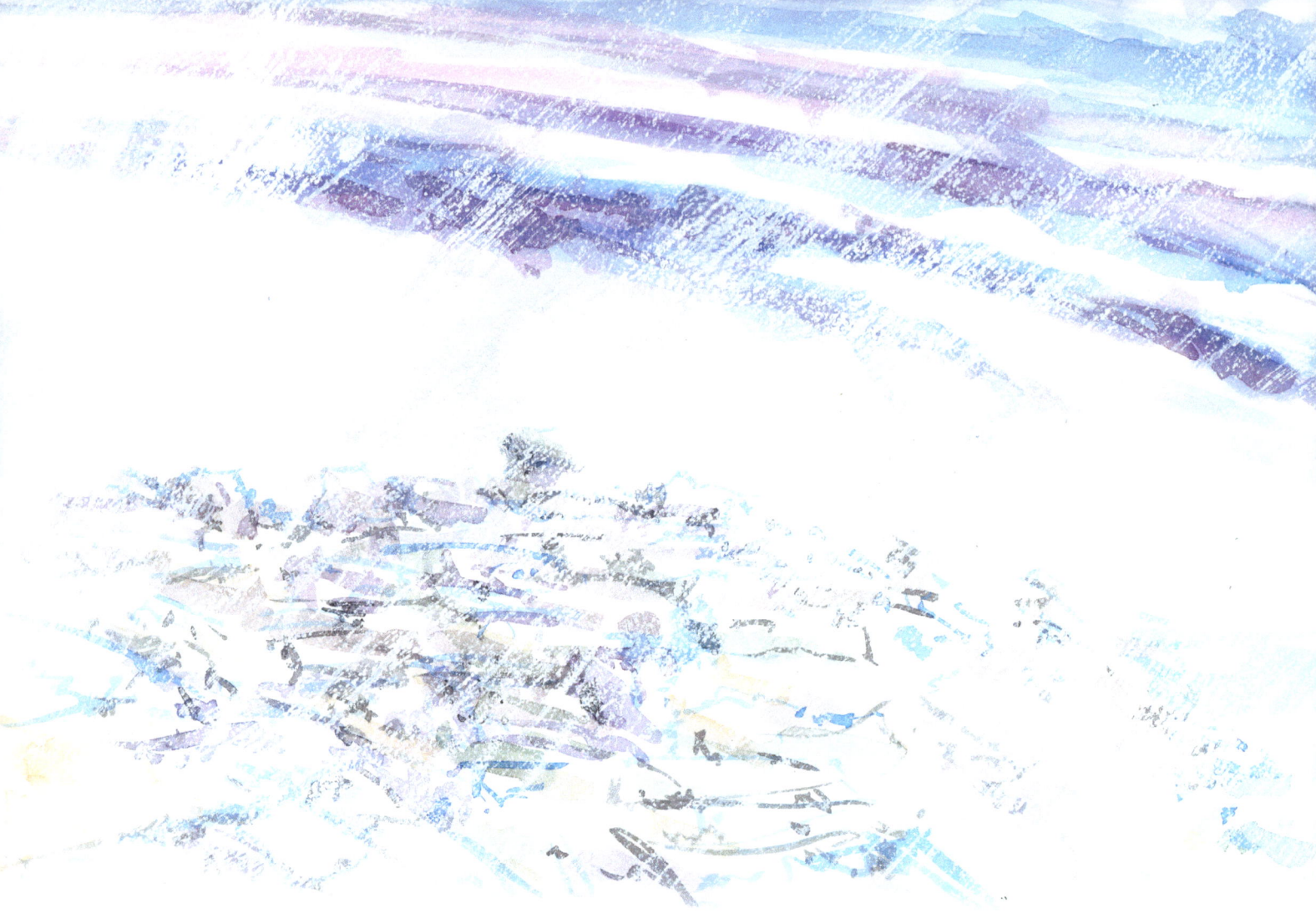

Violent Weather
Watercolour 340 x 540 mm

When at it's worst the weather here is life threatening. On these occasions it is near impossible to cross this landscape on foot or horseback. The driving winds increase the chill factor and visibility is reduced to a minimum. Here there is very little shelter and that what does exist is greatly distanced apart.

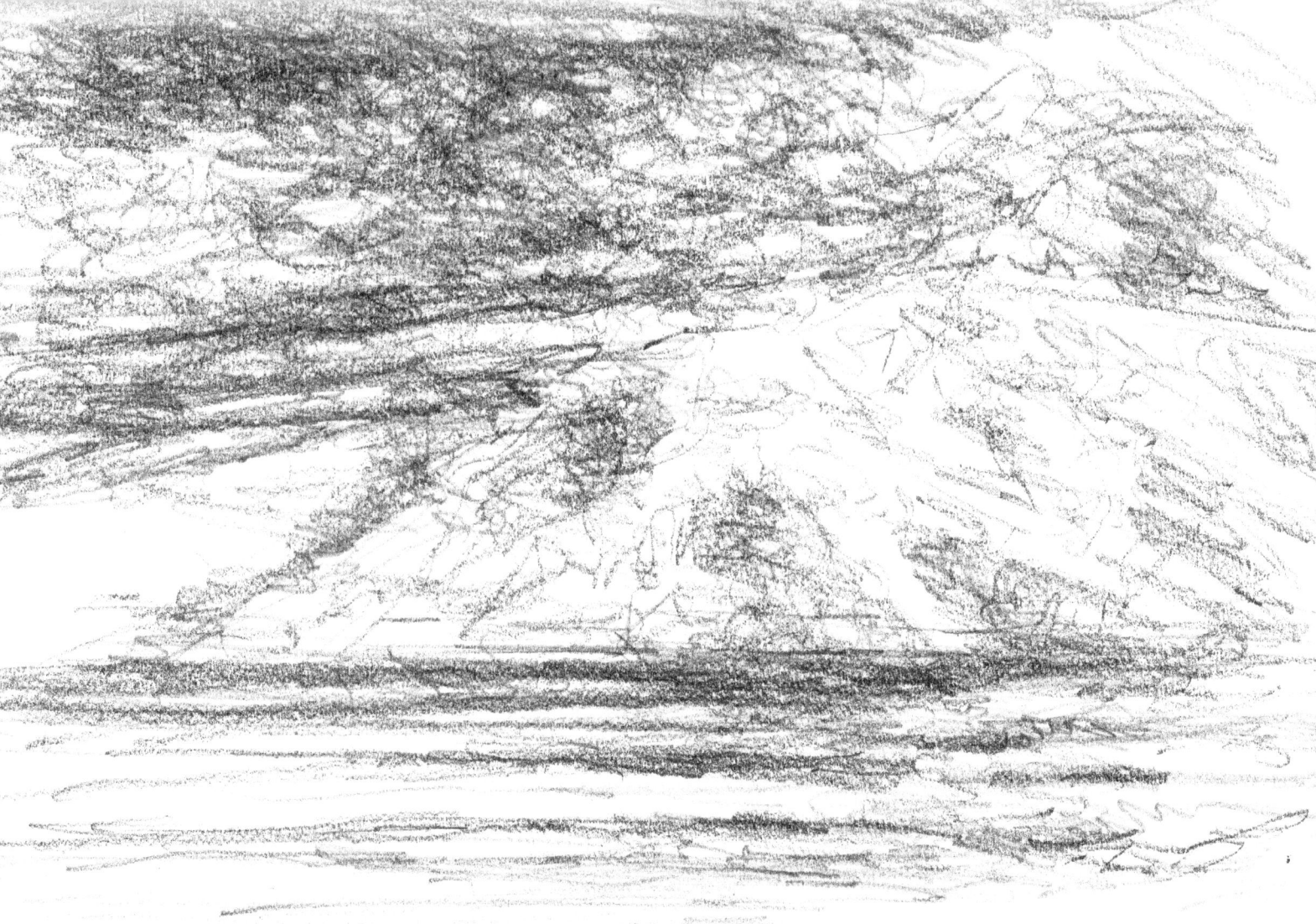

Storm Clouds
Pencil 210 x 297 mm

As winter begins to release it's icy grip upon the moorland and the weather patterns begin to change tremendous storms whip the landscape. At this time of year the cloud formations often resemble an enormous abstract battlefield.

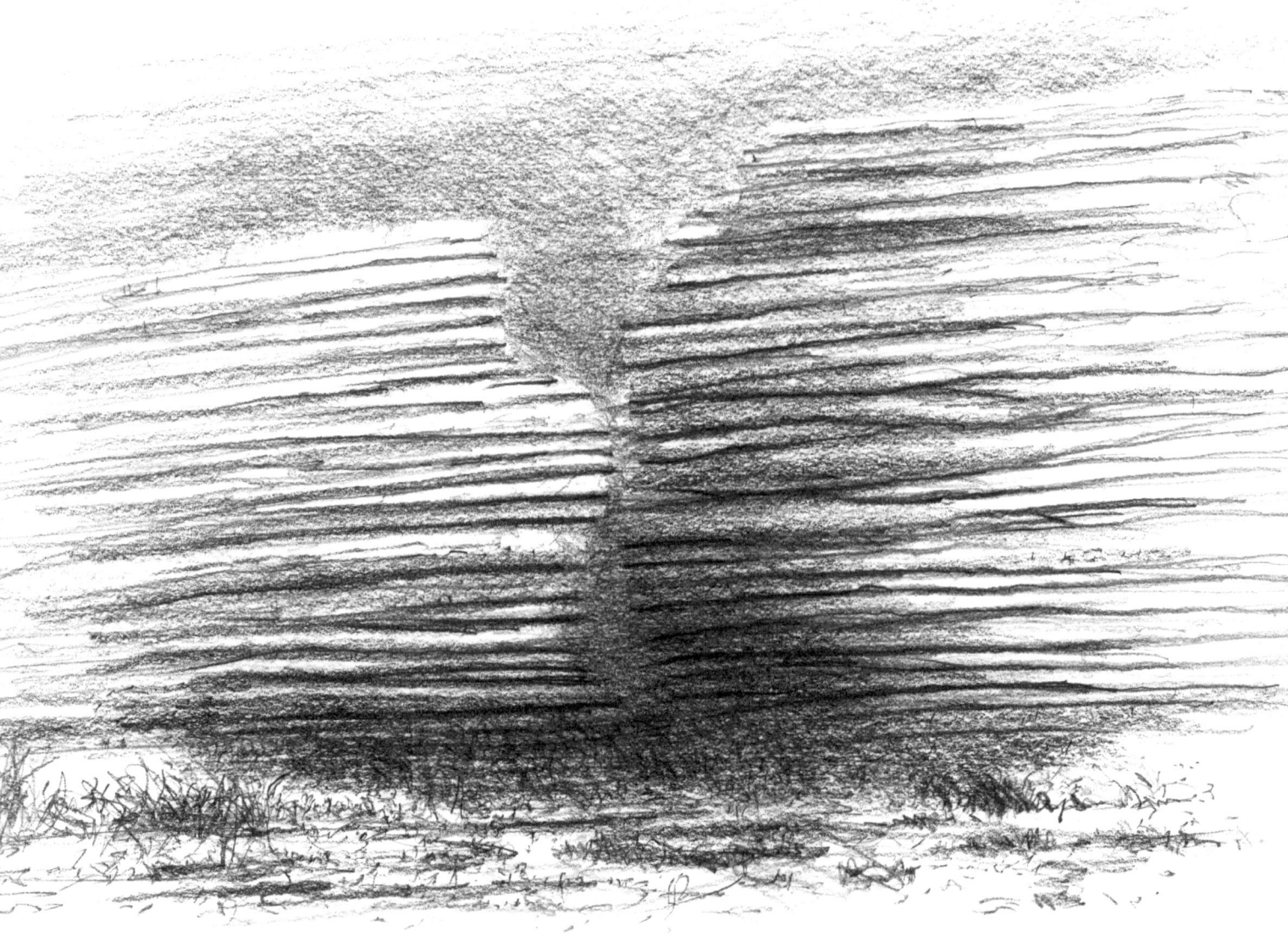

Kissing Rocks
Pencil 290 x 420 mm

The winter at times seems endless, it is as if even the rocks huddle together for comfort. These giants were formed millions of years ago, they were born from the erupting fire from below. They stand to this day as monuments to nature's incredible powers.

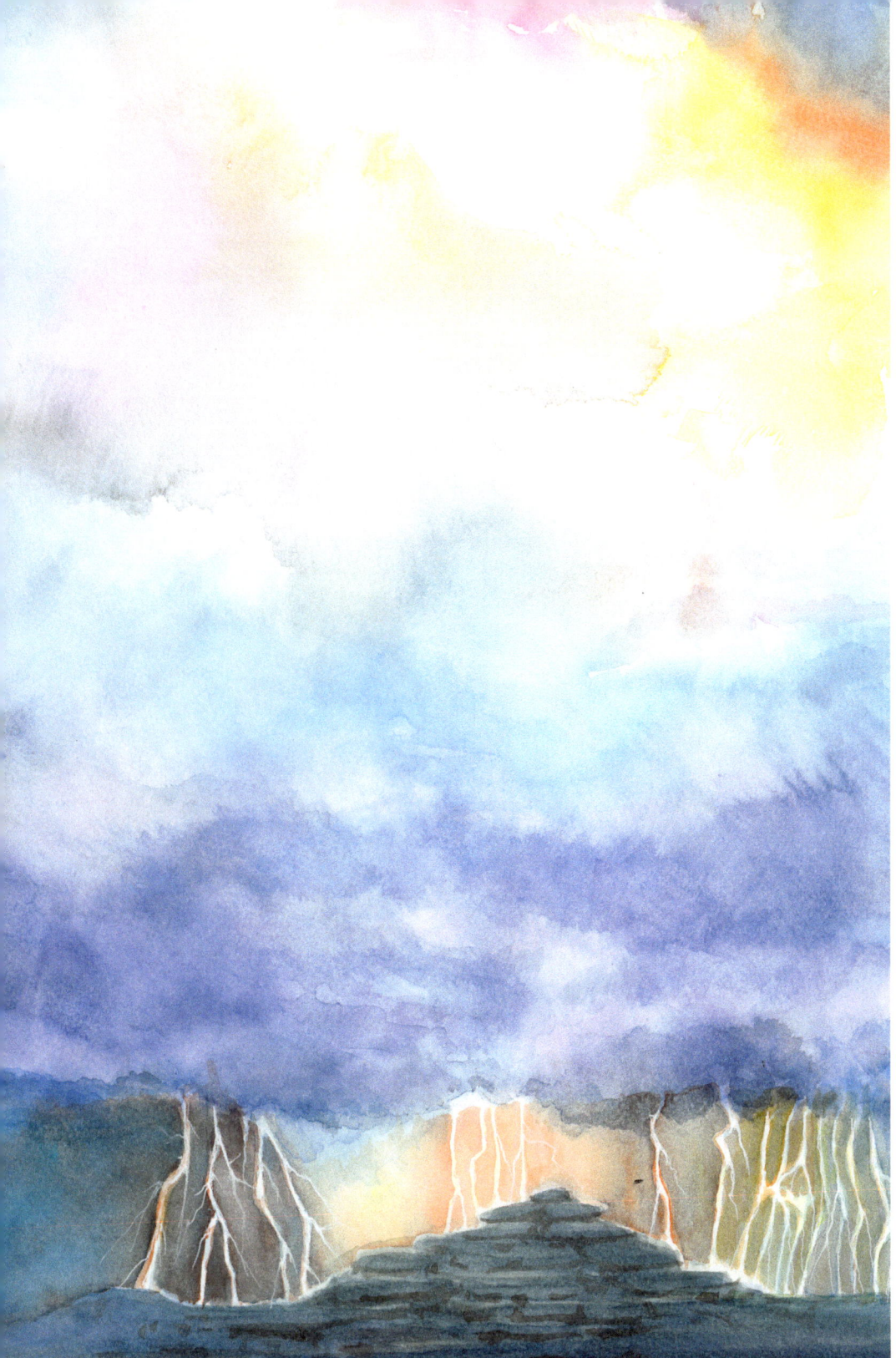

Touch of Fire
Watercolour 540 x 340 mm

As the sky darkens a deep roar comes from the horizon. Birds vacate the sky and the air becomes still. Within a short time this thunder becomes deafeningly amplified and the inevitable storm is directly above. Then nature unleashes yet another wonder. Raw energy is dispensed from the sky and massive fiery fingers touch the ground below.

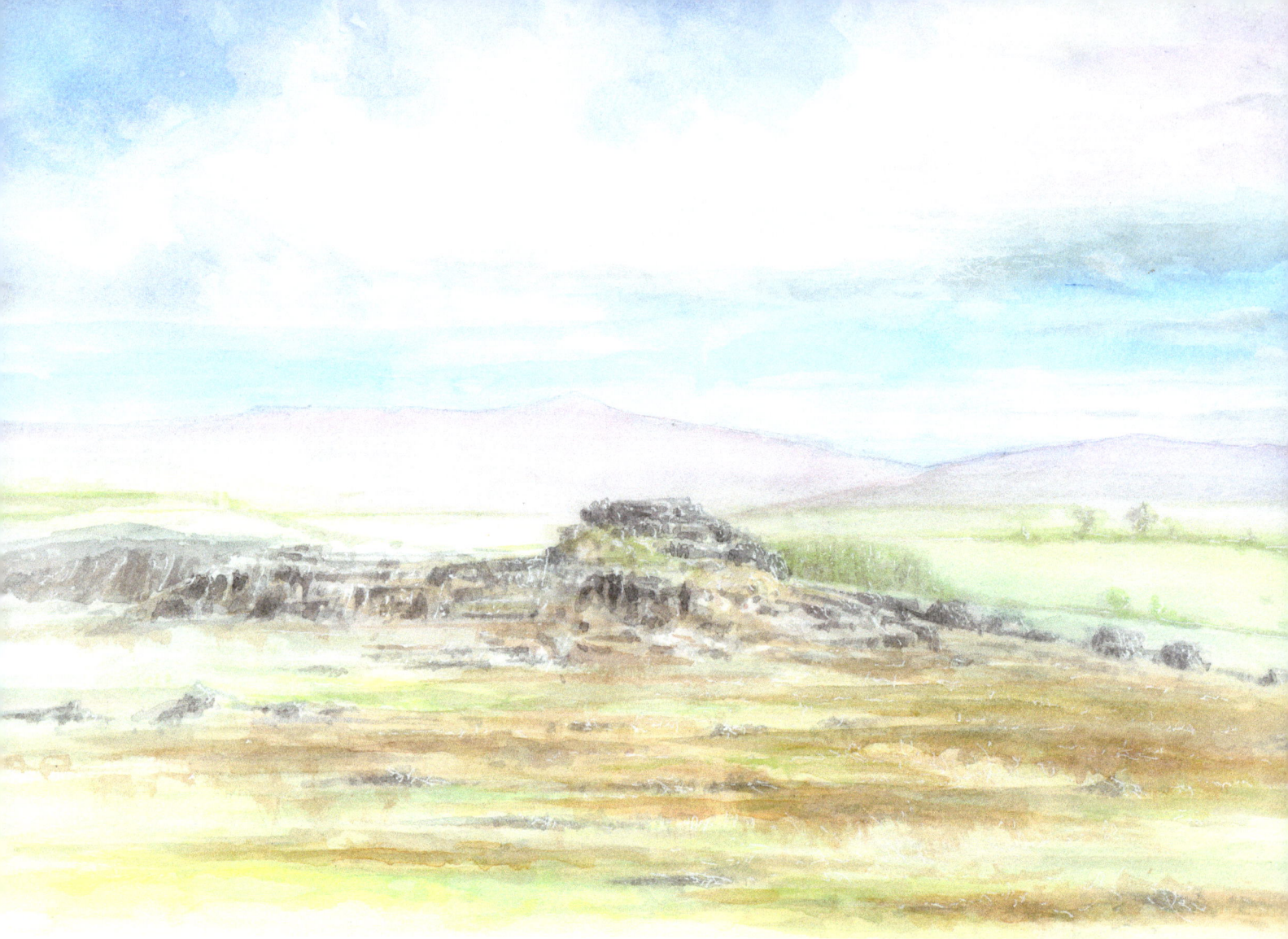

Signs of Spring
Watercolour 340 x 540 mm

The herald of awakening arrives and springtime signals all life to emerge. No day of the year is more wondrous than that on which spring finally arrives. It is a time of cleanliness, a time with a unique smell of it's own, a time of renewal and promise.

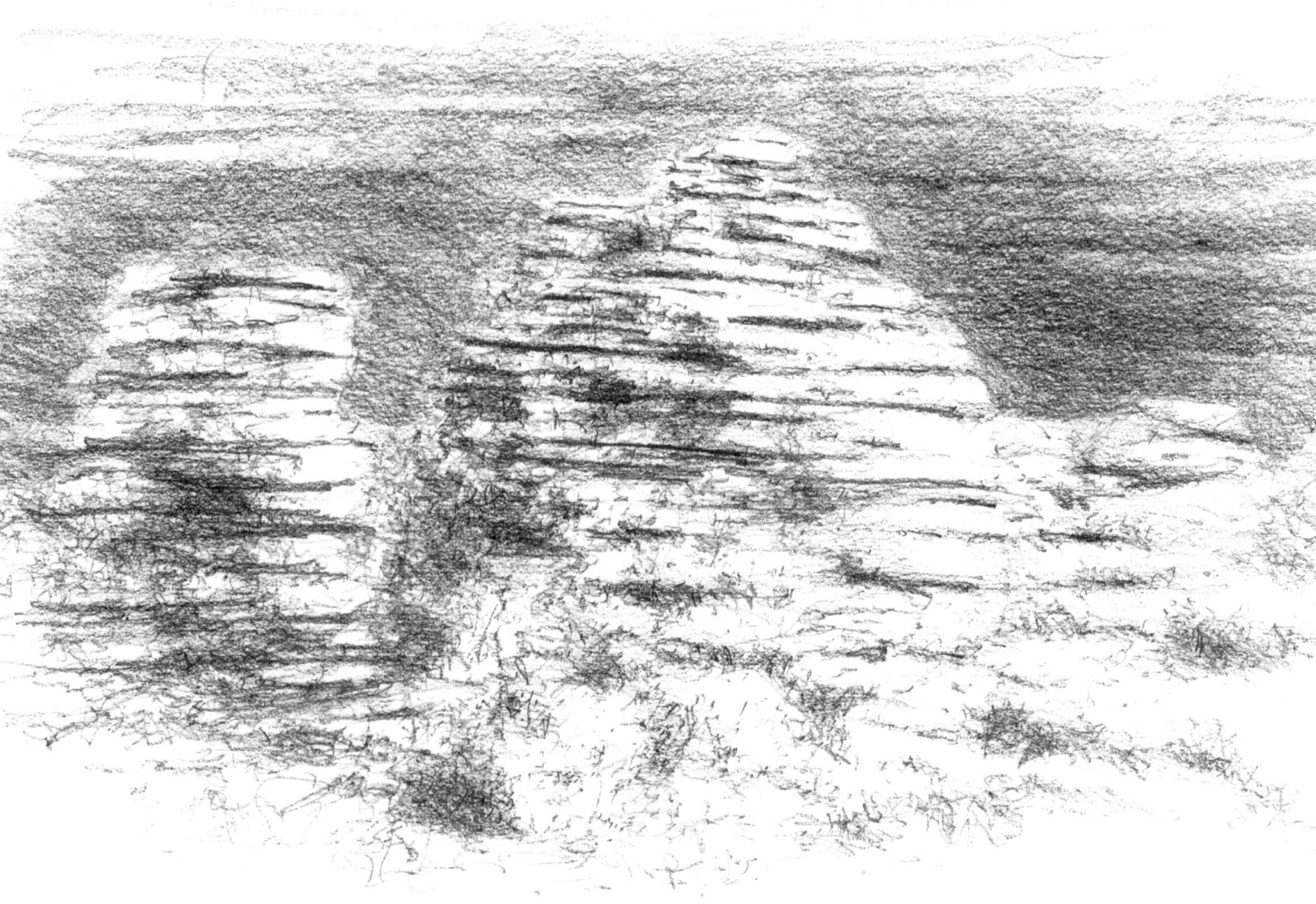

Erect Giants
Pencil 290 x 420 mm

As all living things begin to rejuvenate it is as though even the rock formations become more erect. Due to the durability and magnificence of these giants it is little wonder that early humankind thought of them as being spiritual signifiers.

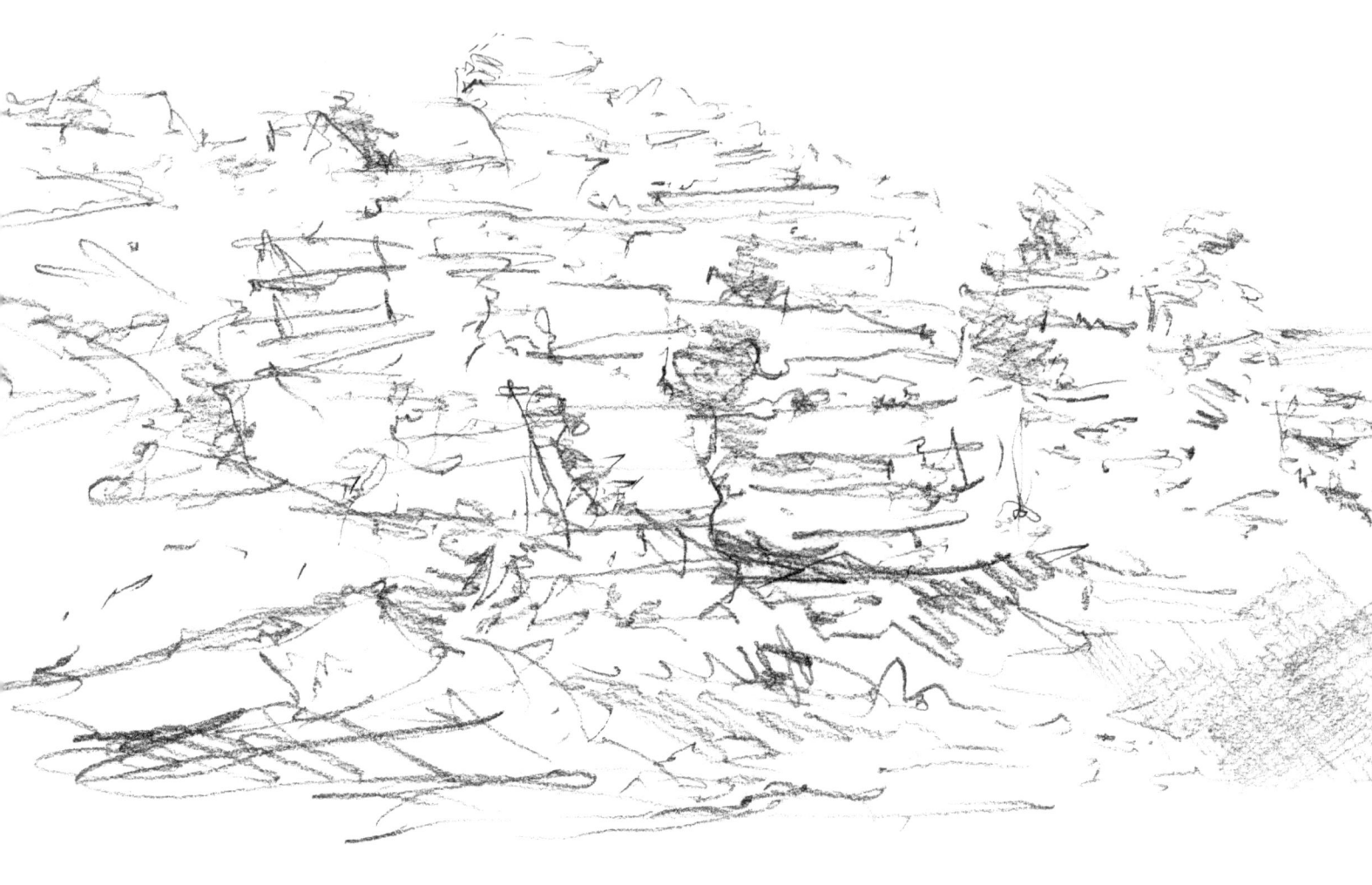

Quiet Family
Pencil 290 x 420 mm

These mounds of mineral deposits evolved at exactly the same time and are therefore closely related. In the sunshine they seem to quietly relax and enjoy the company of each other. Inanimate they may be but they are as integral to life on this planet as is anything else.

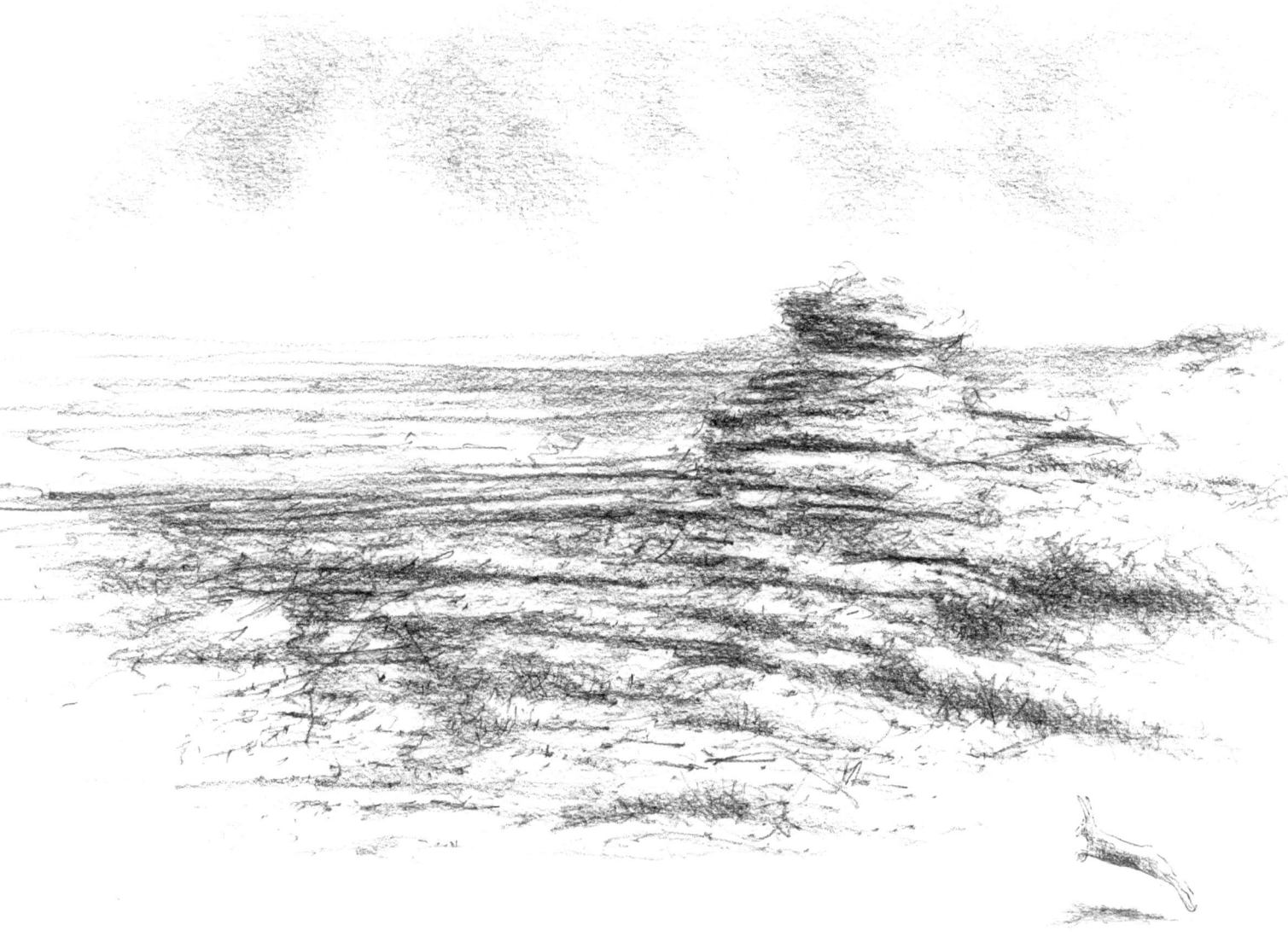

The Orphan
Pencil 290 x 420 mm

Sadly some rocks stand alone. It maybe that their isolation gives them an independence, even possibly an authority. In springtime these lonely statutes preside over and witness nature's drive for new life.

Father & Son
Pencil 290 x 420 mm

Bold Fox [Bottom Right]
Pencil 200 x 200 mm

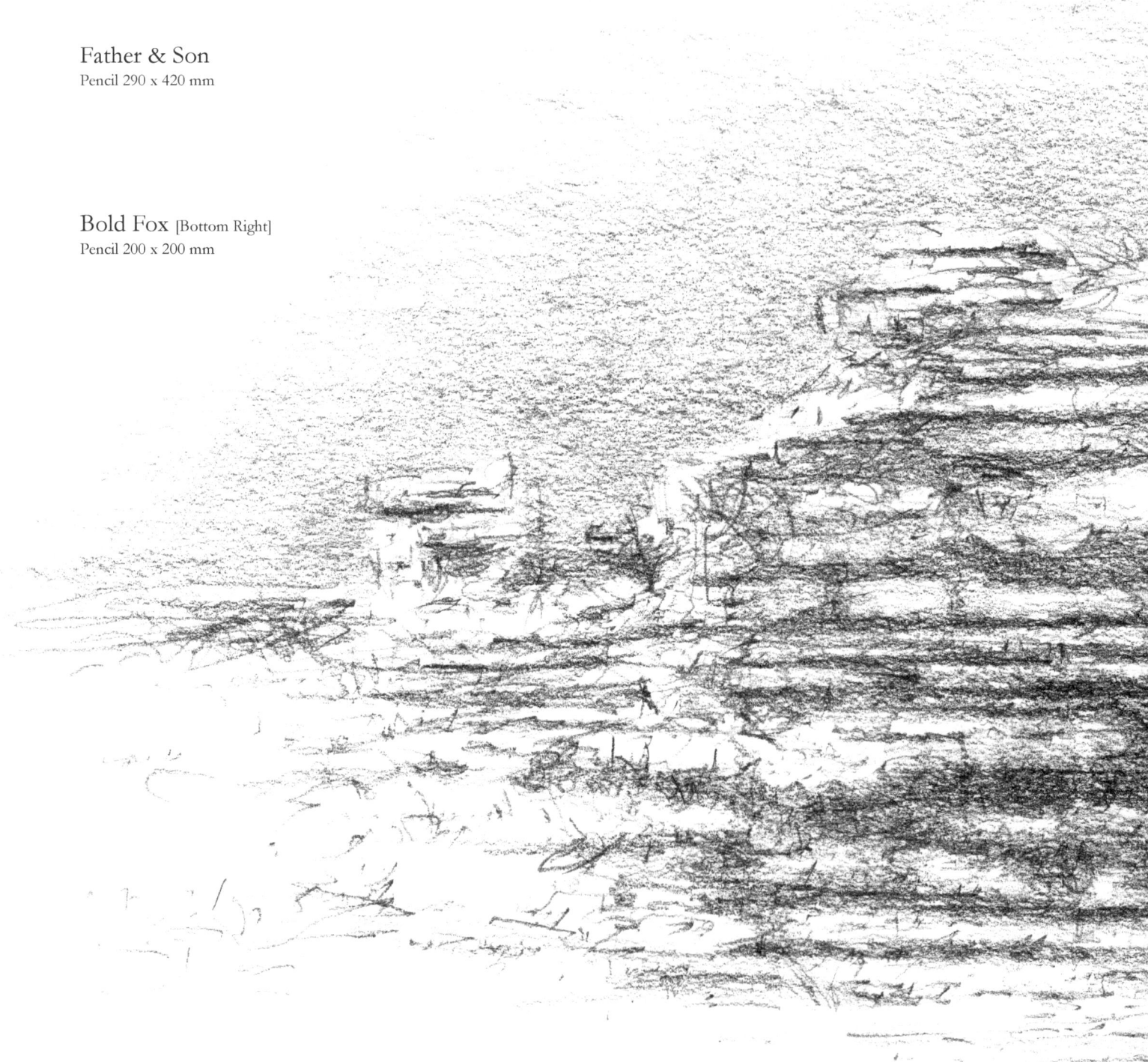

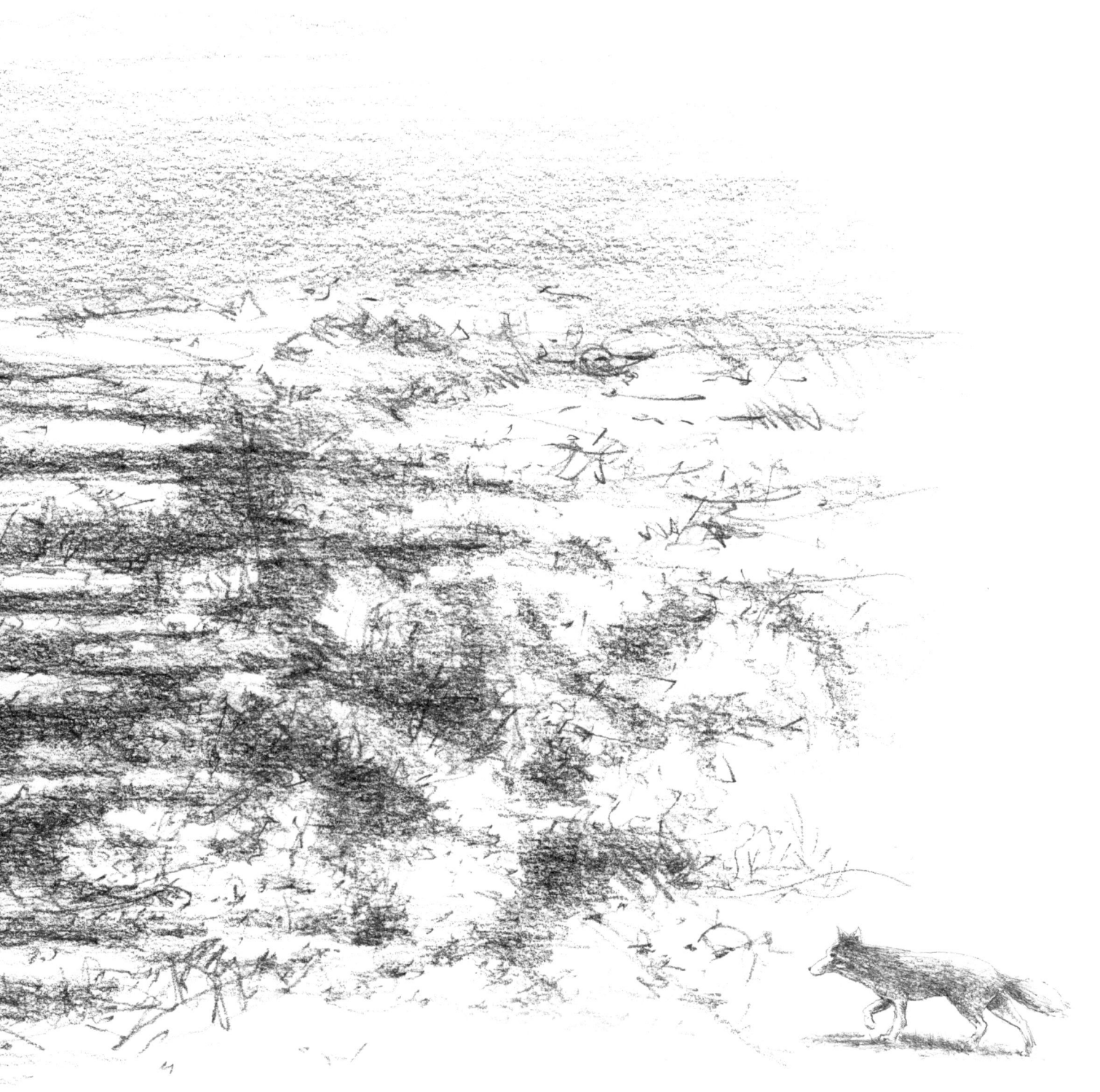

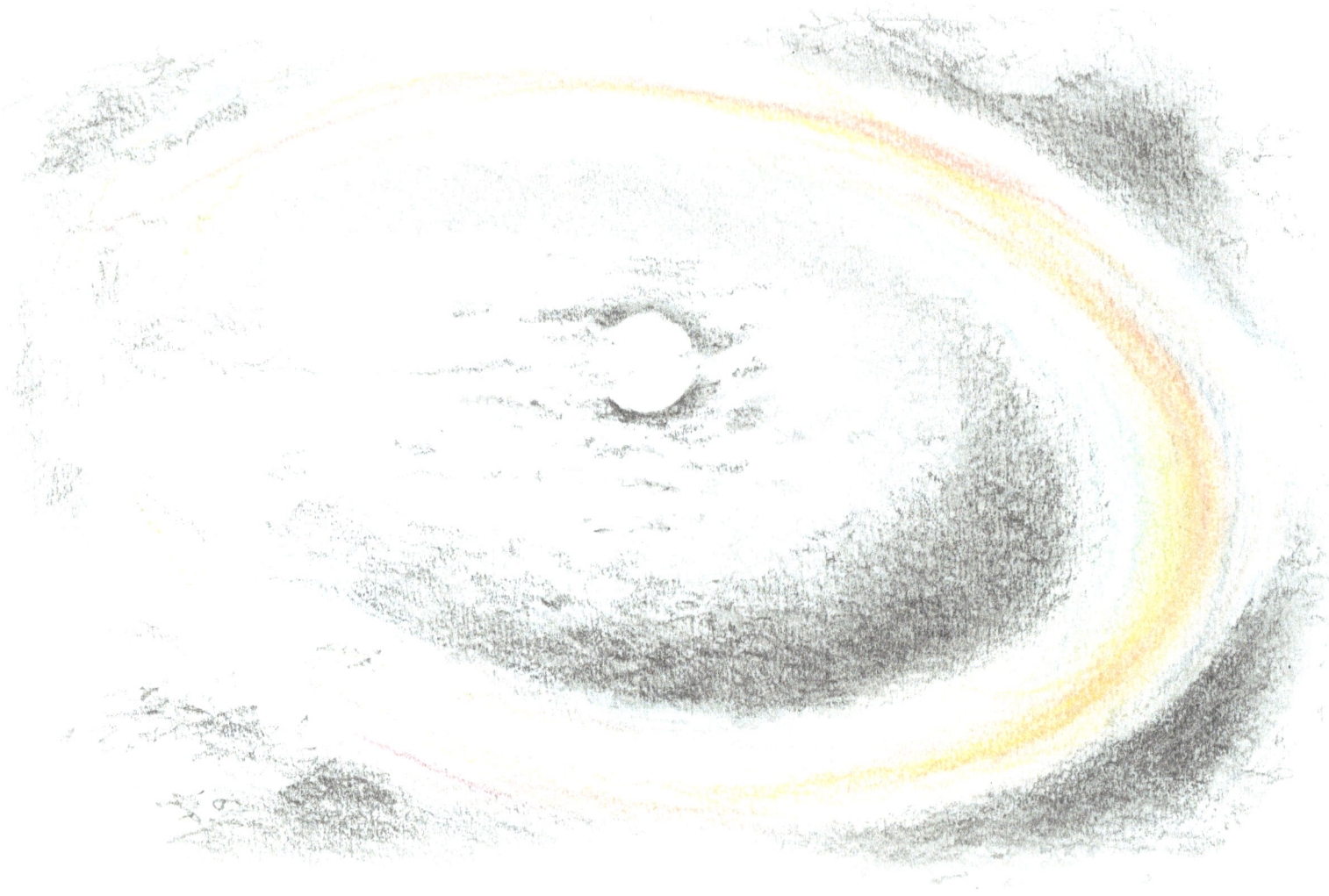

Halo [Page Left]
Pencil 210 x 297 mm

Silver Lining [Page Right]
Watercolour 420 x 290 mm

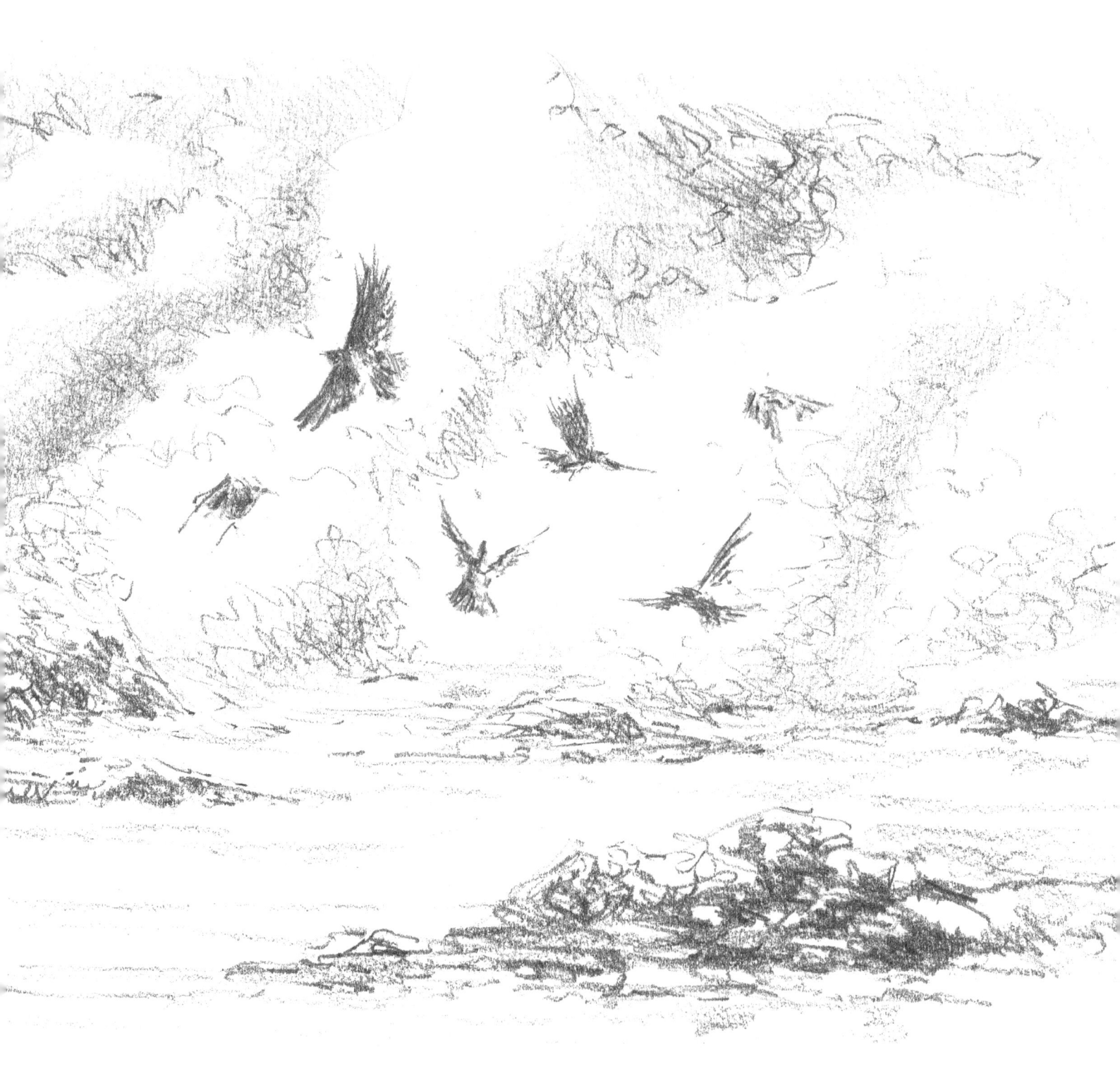

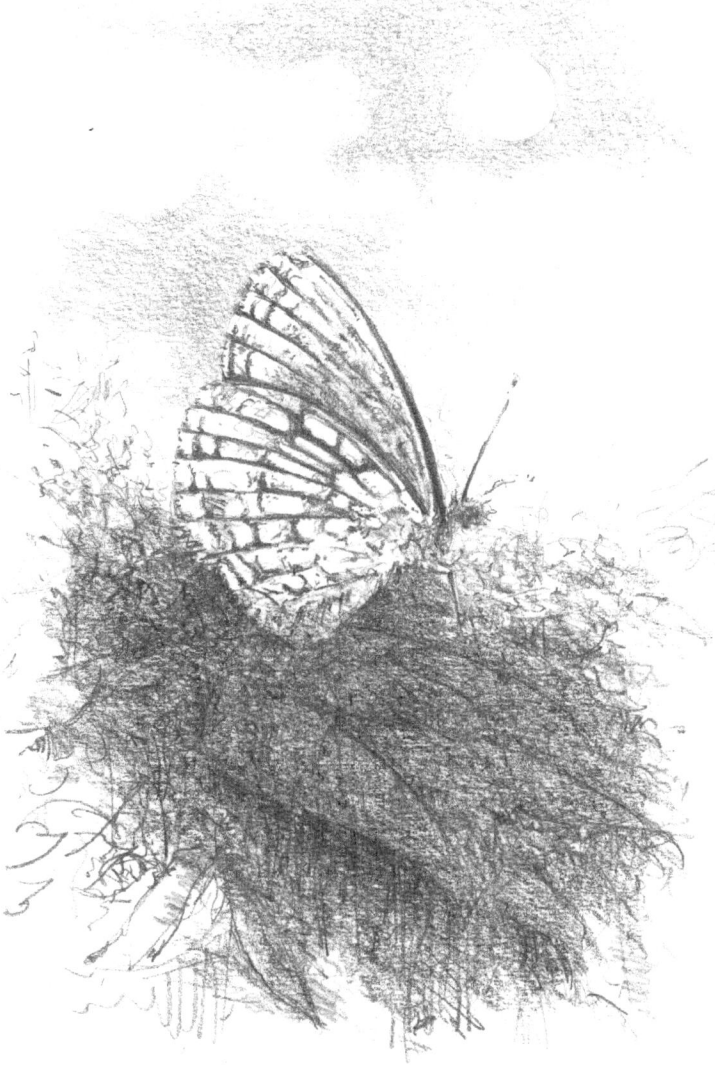

Late Spring [Top Left]
Pencil 297 x 210 mm

Rooks Disturbed [Bottom Right]
Pencil 210 x 210 mm

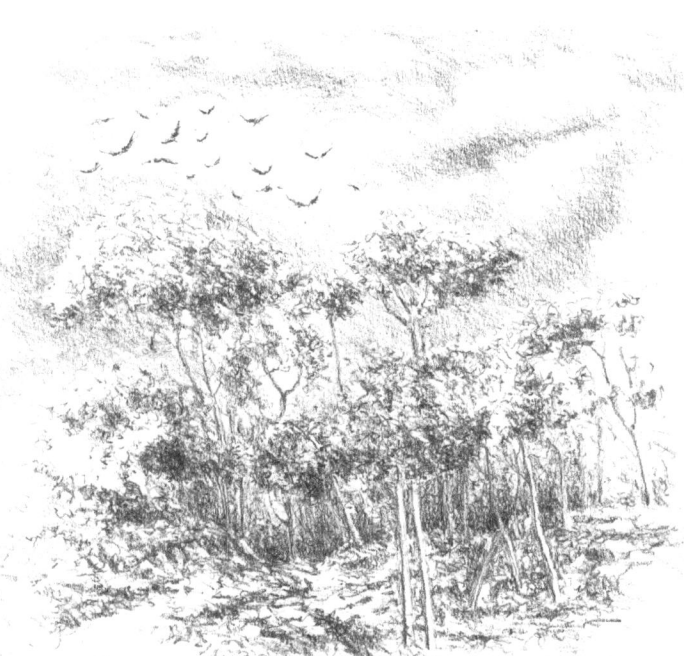

Half Dozen Crows [Page Left]
Pencil 210 x 297 mm

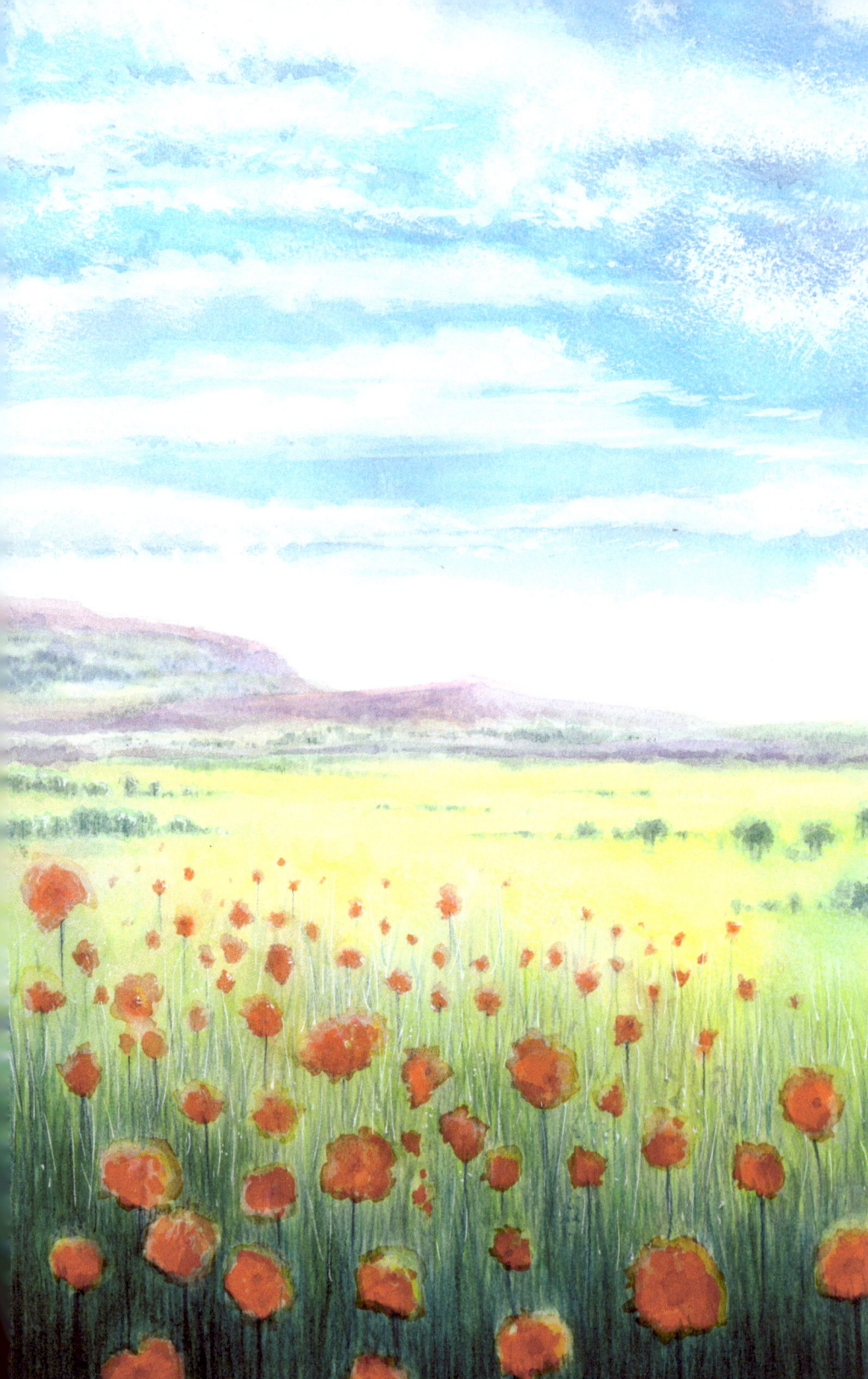

Poppy Fields
Watercolour 540 x 340 mm

Summer eventually arrives and
the moorlands become ablaze
with colour. The innocence and
anticipation of spring has passed
and the full glory and vibrancy
of summertime dominates the
landscape. Long lush days fill the
weeks and new life abounds.

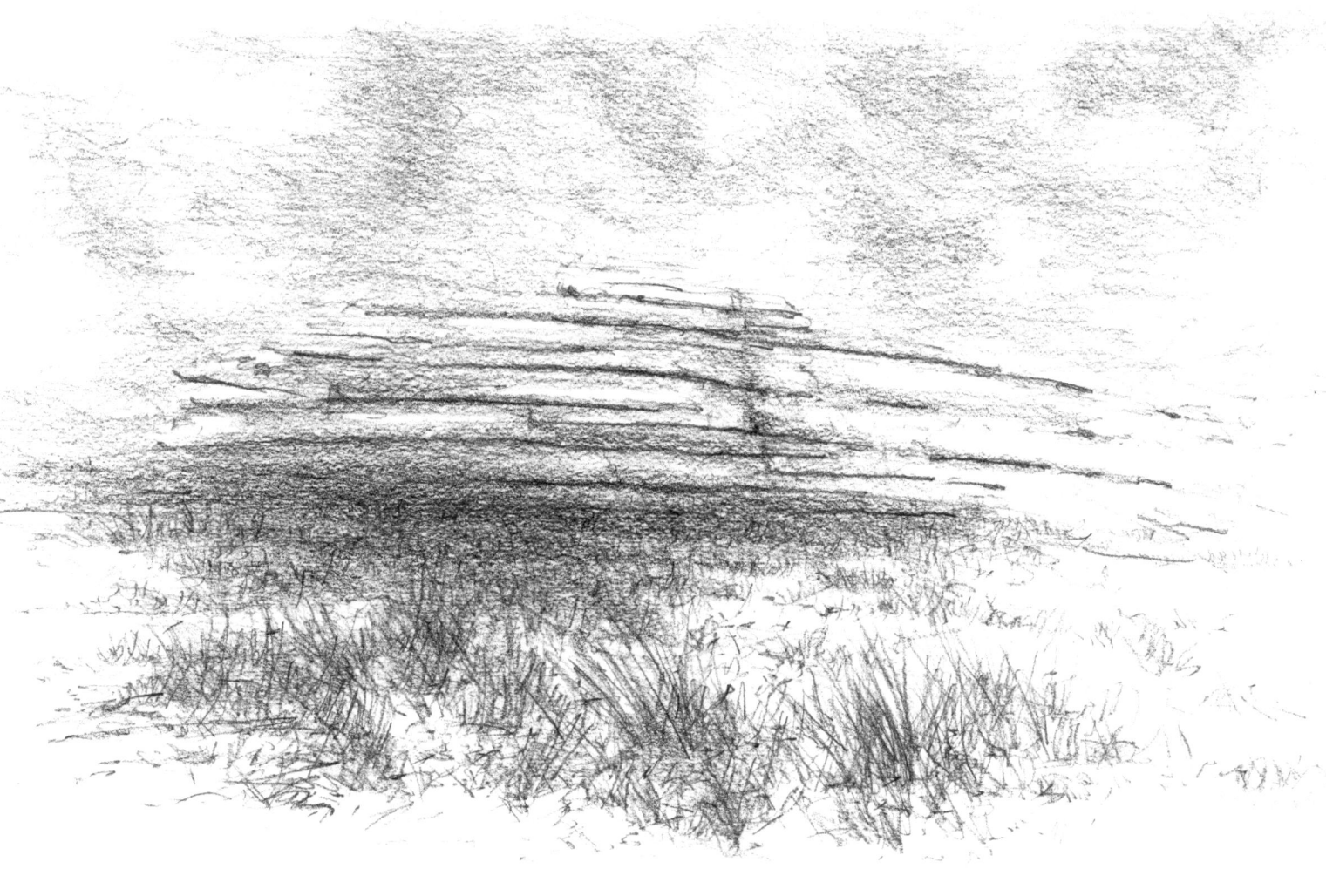

Summer Grasses
Pencil 290 x 420 mm

The summer grasses reach their full height and wildflowers carpet the landscape.
The majestic Tors cast deep purple shadows over this orchestra of growth.

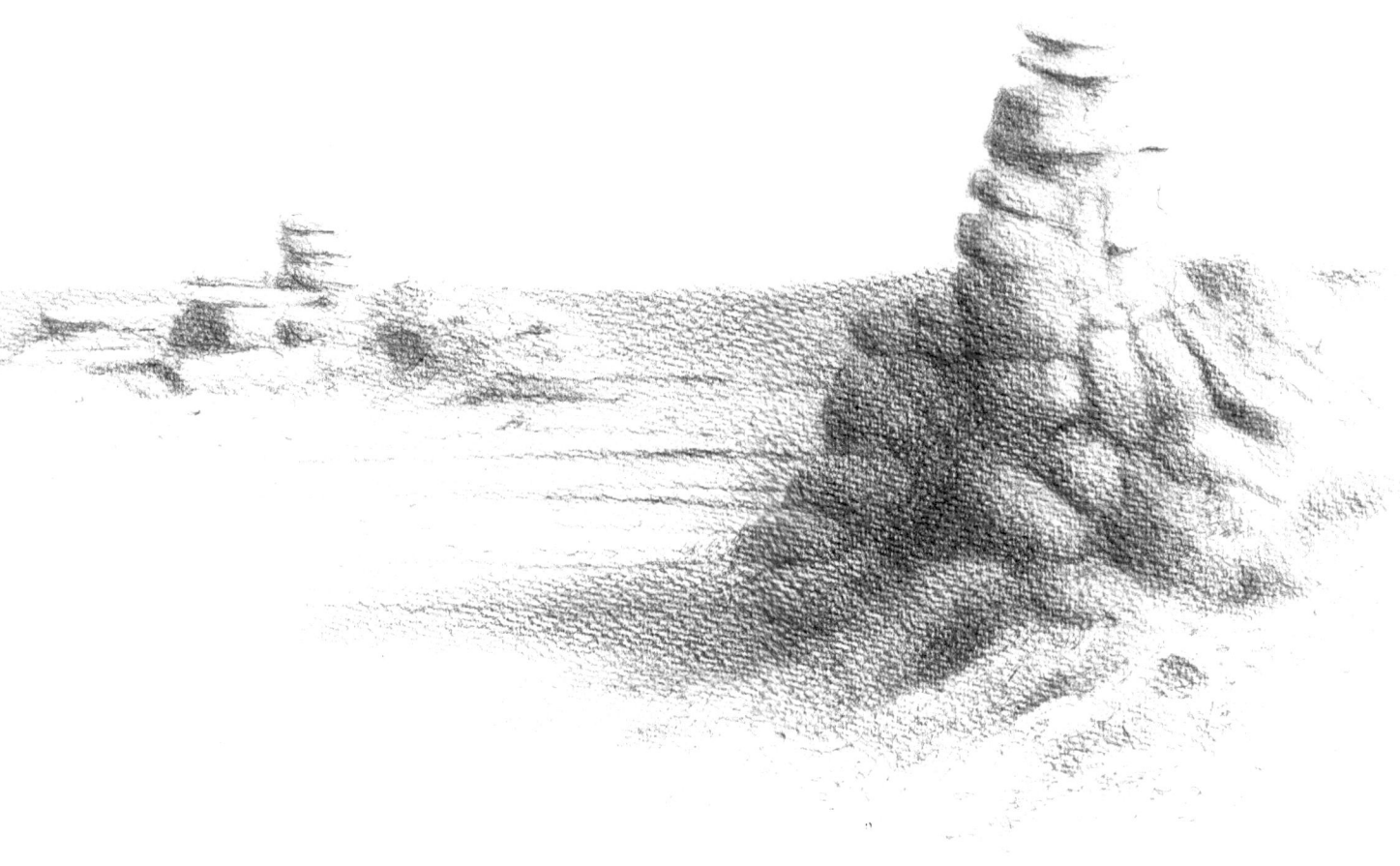

Chess Pieces
Pencil 300 x 500 mm

When the sun reaches it's zenith during summer the Tors appear to take on a new identity. Their language is not audible to us but language they do possess. Their movements go unnoticed by human eyes but move they do. This almost silent secret mobility can only be witnessed over millions of years.

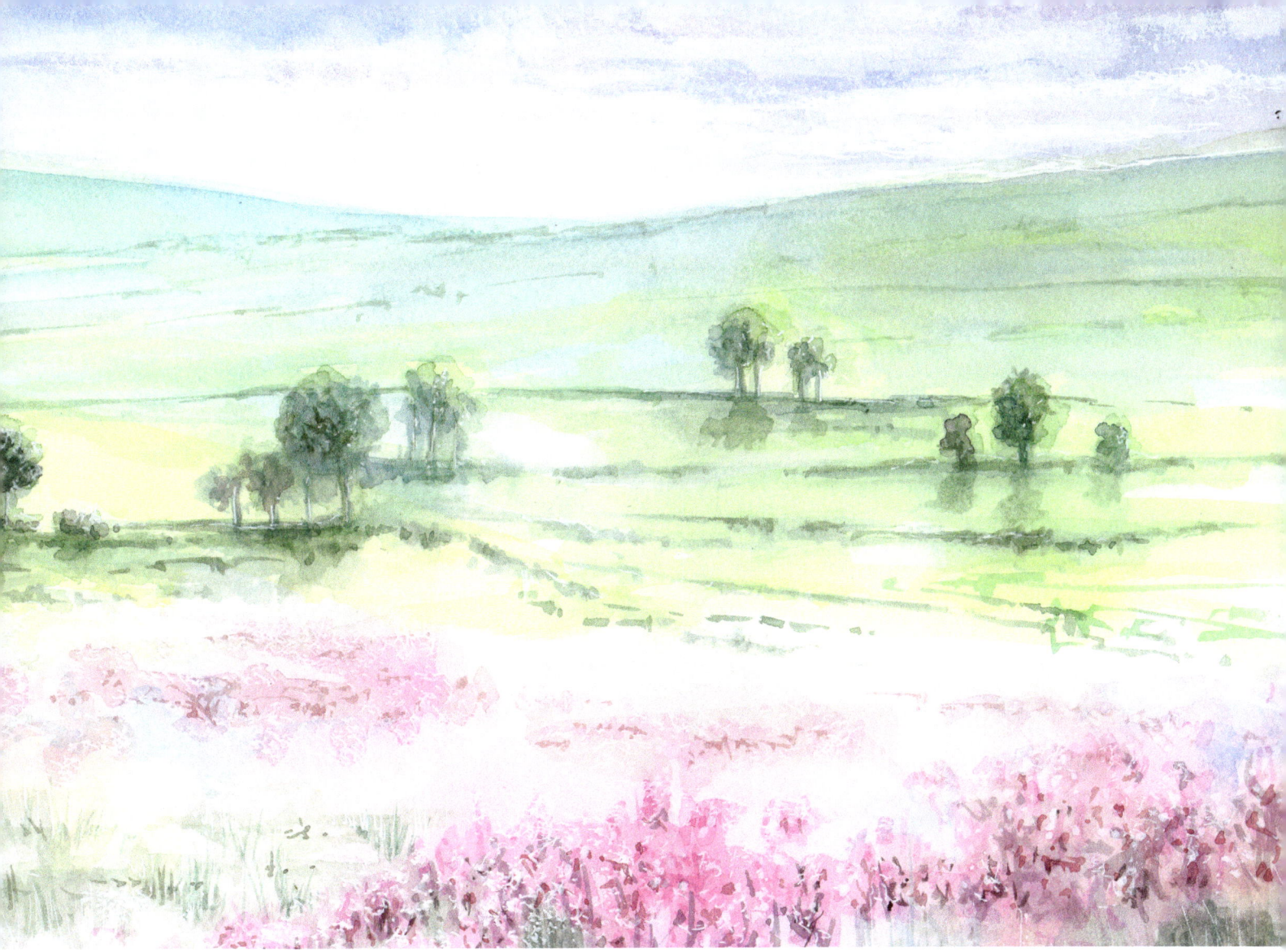

Summer Carpet
Watercolour 340 x 540 mm

In winter this landscape offers little shelter from the cold and wet weather. During days of intense heat the same applies. Tall rocks and trees afford shade but they are often far apart. Colourful and beautiful as this place maybe it is apparent why it remains very much uninhabited by humans.

Fly-By Butterfly [Mid Left]
Pencil 200 x 200 mm

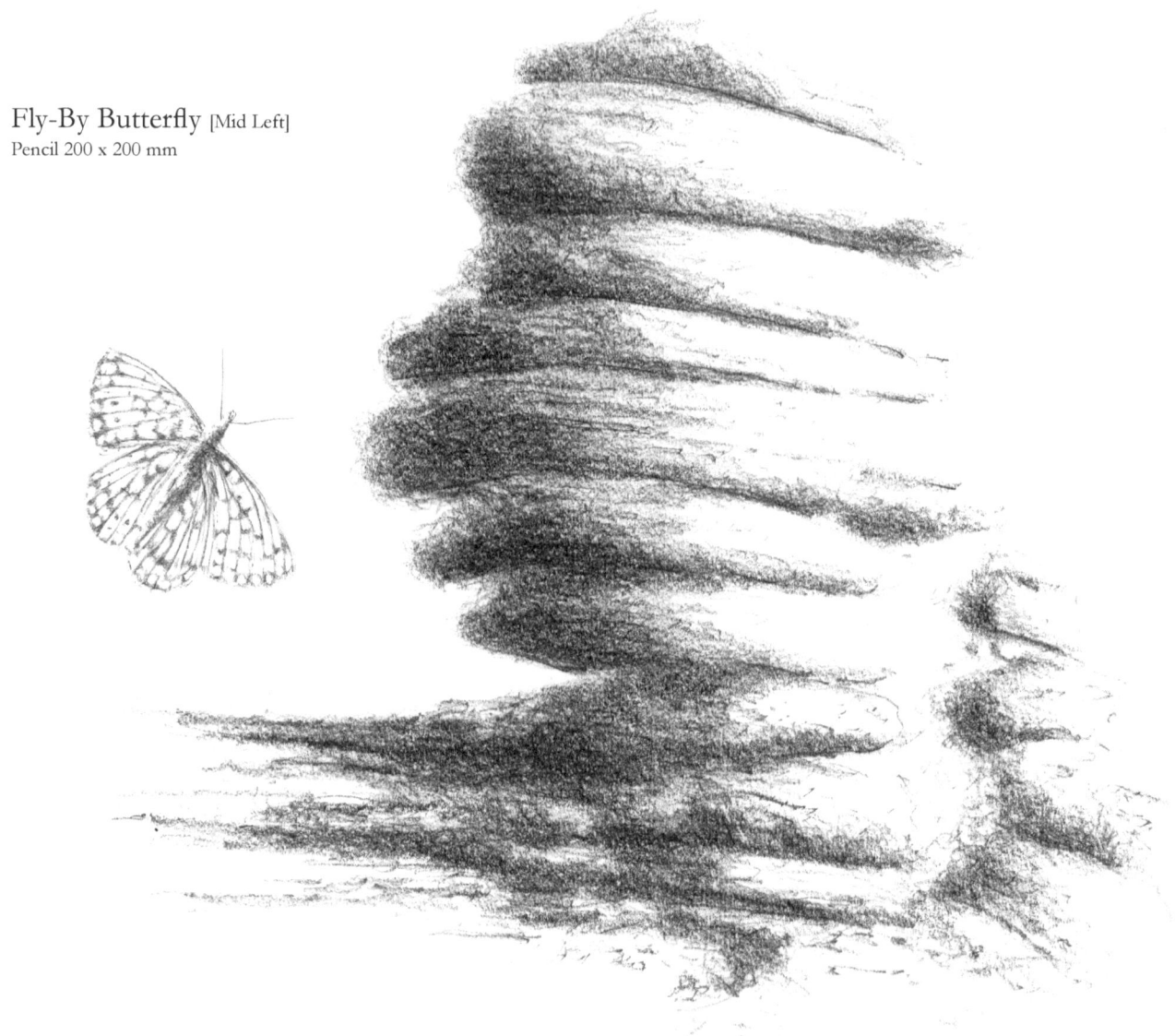

Day in a Million [Centre]
Pencil 290 x 420 mm

These petrified monuments are so peculiar that it is difficult to believe that they were not constructed by human beings. In fact they originated at the time that this planet was born. Molten rock erupted from beneath and the cold moist air sculpted the Tors. These glorious relics remain to document the birth of Planet Earth.

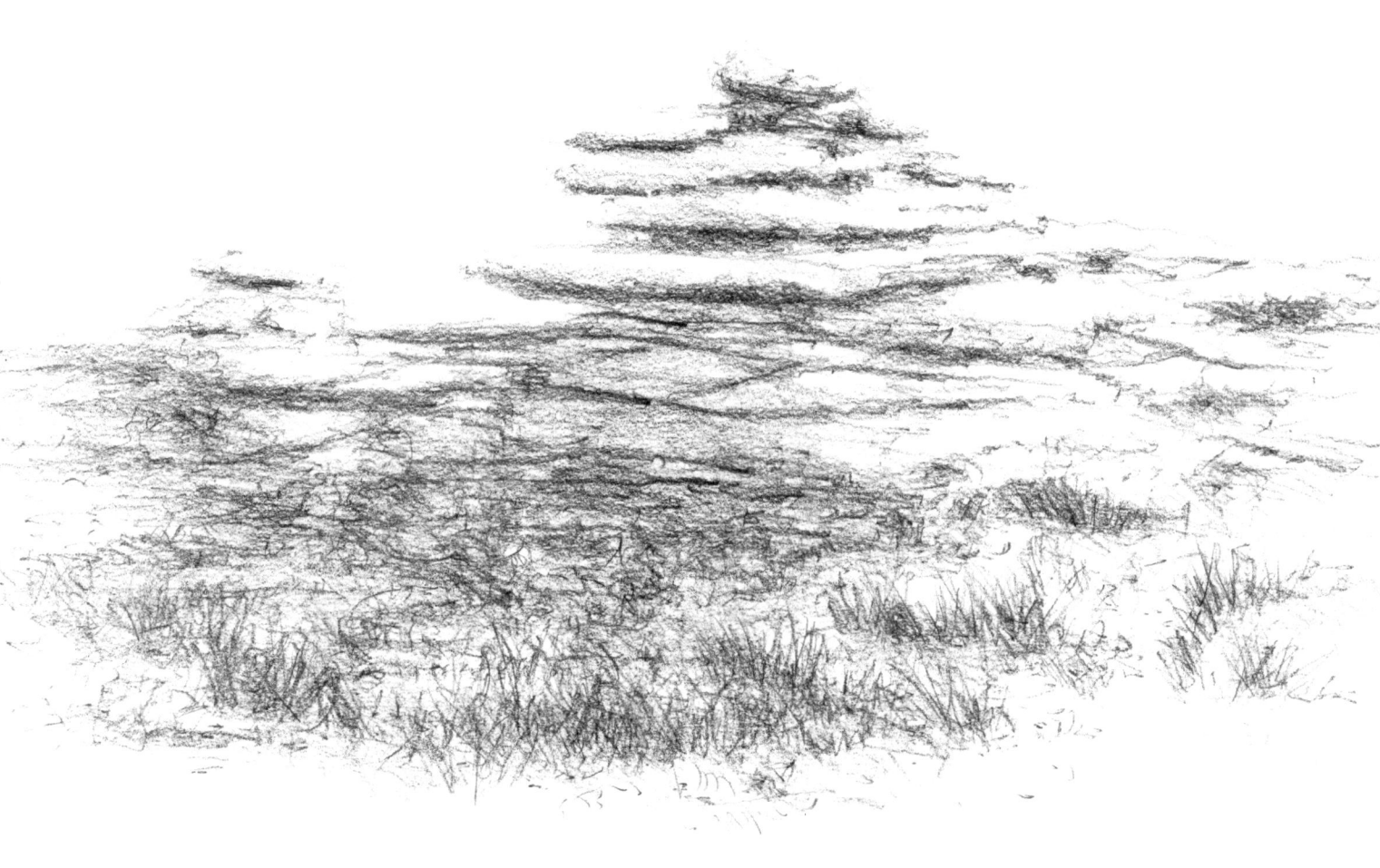

Talking Rocks
Pencil 290 x 420 mm

Summertime reintroduces many somewhat familiar aspects of humankind's experiences. Our senses are bombarded by the intense scents of summer while the subtle sounds of birdsong and insects fill the air. How much more is there that is all around us that we can neither smell or hear?

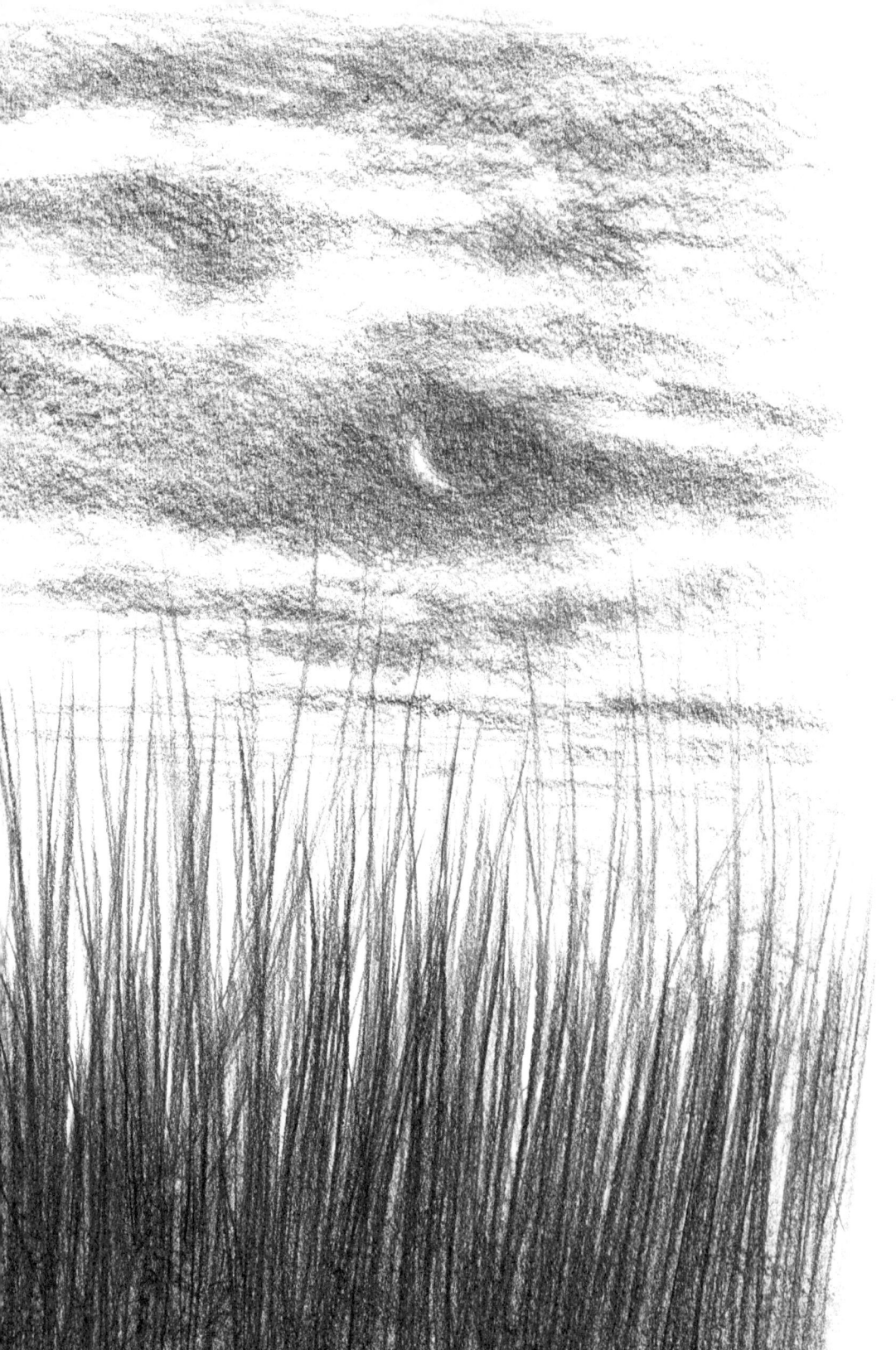

Crescent Moon & Grasses
Pencil 420 x 290 mm

The evening delivers a welcome
cool breeze and the long grasses
provide a soft and comfortable
resting place. To be under the
heavens on a warm dry night is
something most of us have
almost forgotten. Here is a
perfect place and time to
not think.

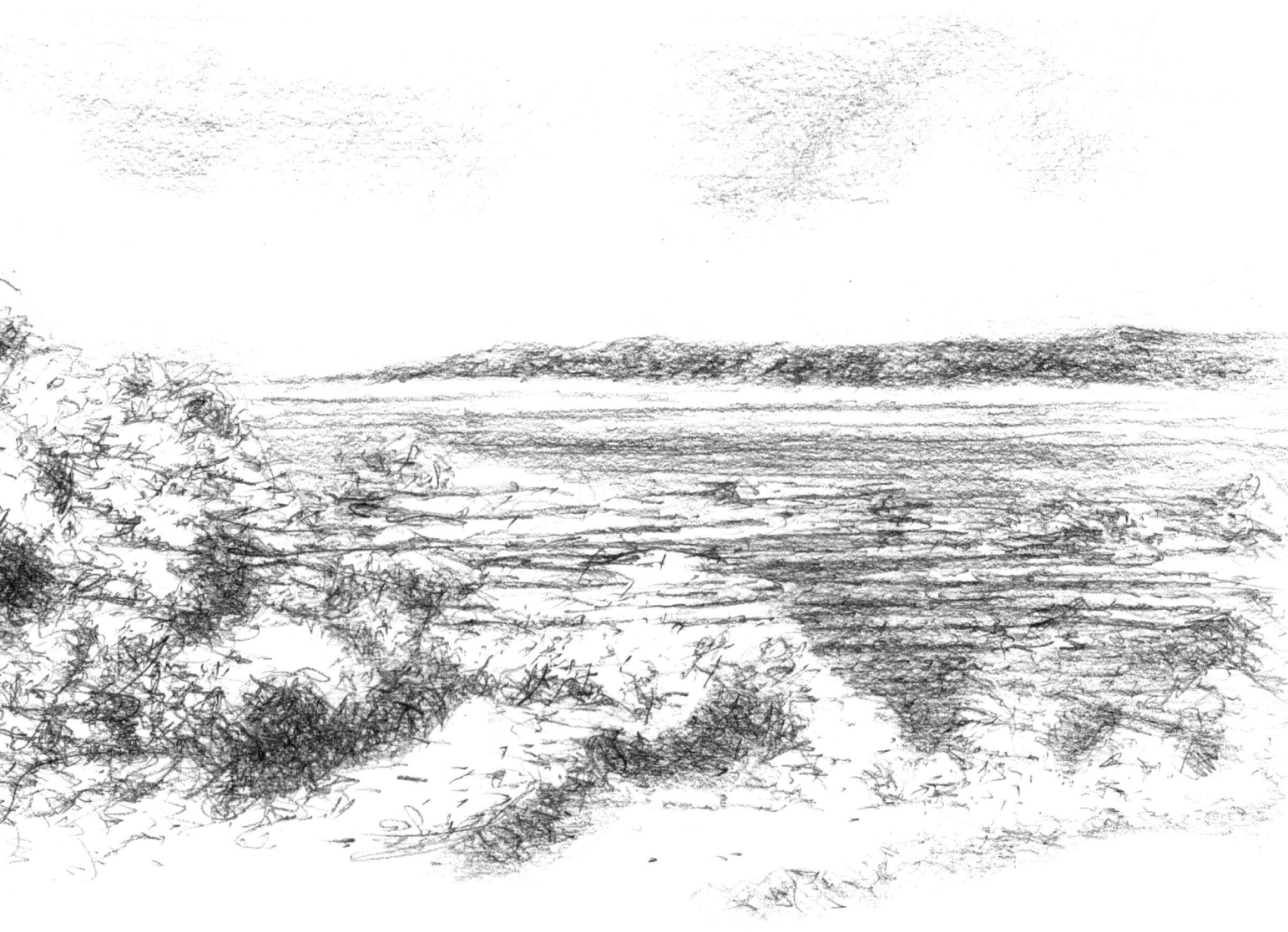

Sun Kissed Valley
Pencil 290 x 420 mm

The sun takes charge very early in the day at this time of year. Daybreak begins with a clear sky and warm air. The promise of a high temperature is evident. Most of the activity that will take place on the landscape today will occur long before midday. We often yearn for the sun to kiss the earth but sometimes we pray for rain.

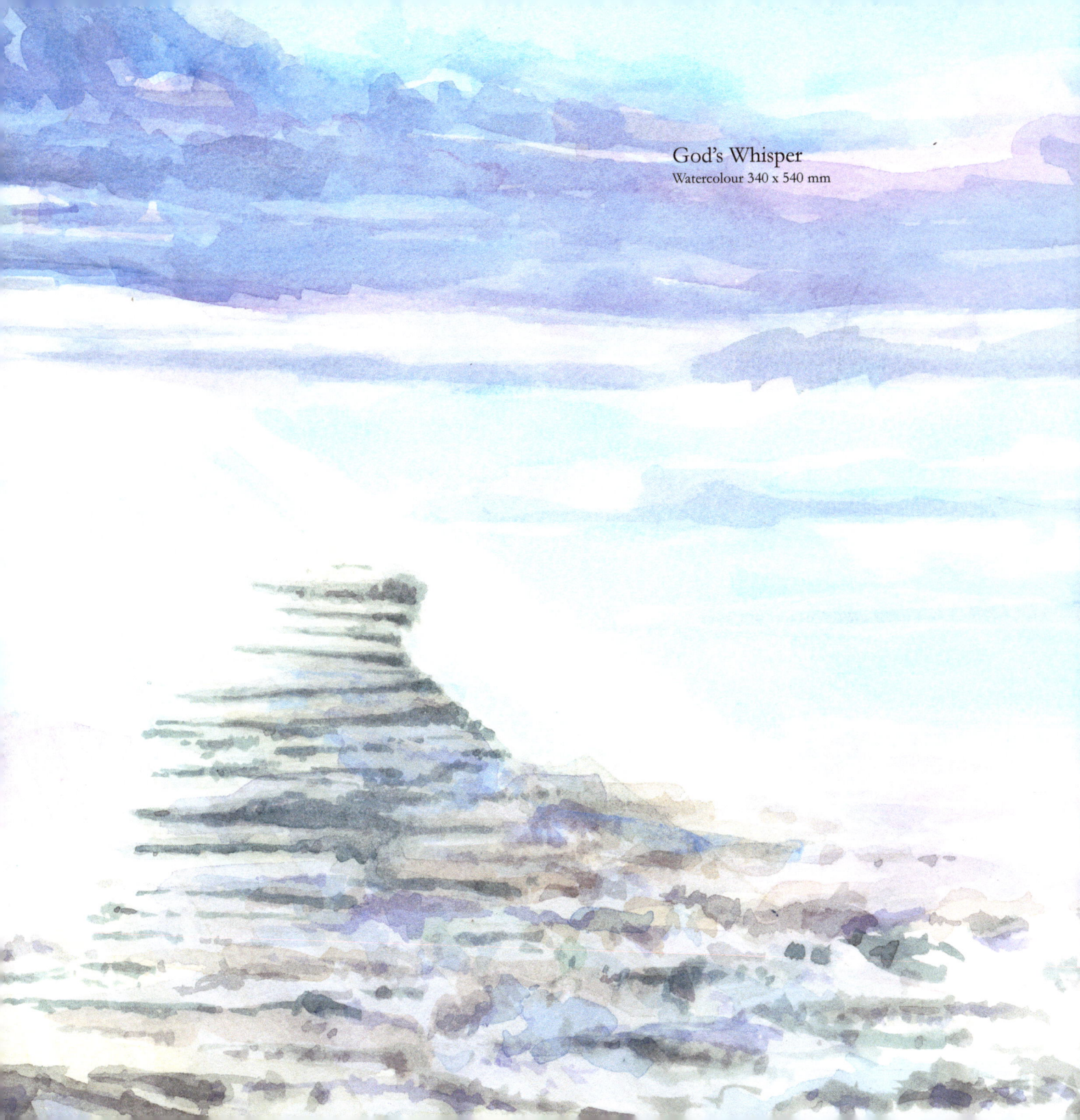

God's Whisper
Watercolour 340 x 540 mm

Snuggling Giants
Pencil 290 x 420 mm

The shape and form of the Tors is diverse indeed. Seen through a heat haze they appear to shimmer and shake. It is almost as though they were breathing, Maybe they are!

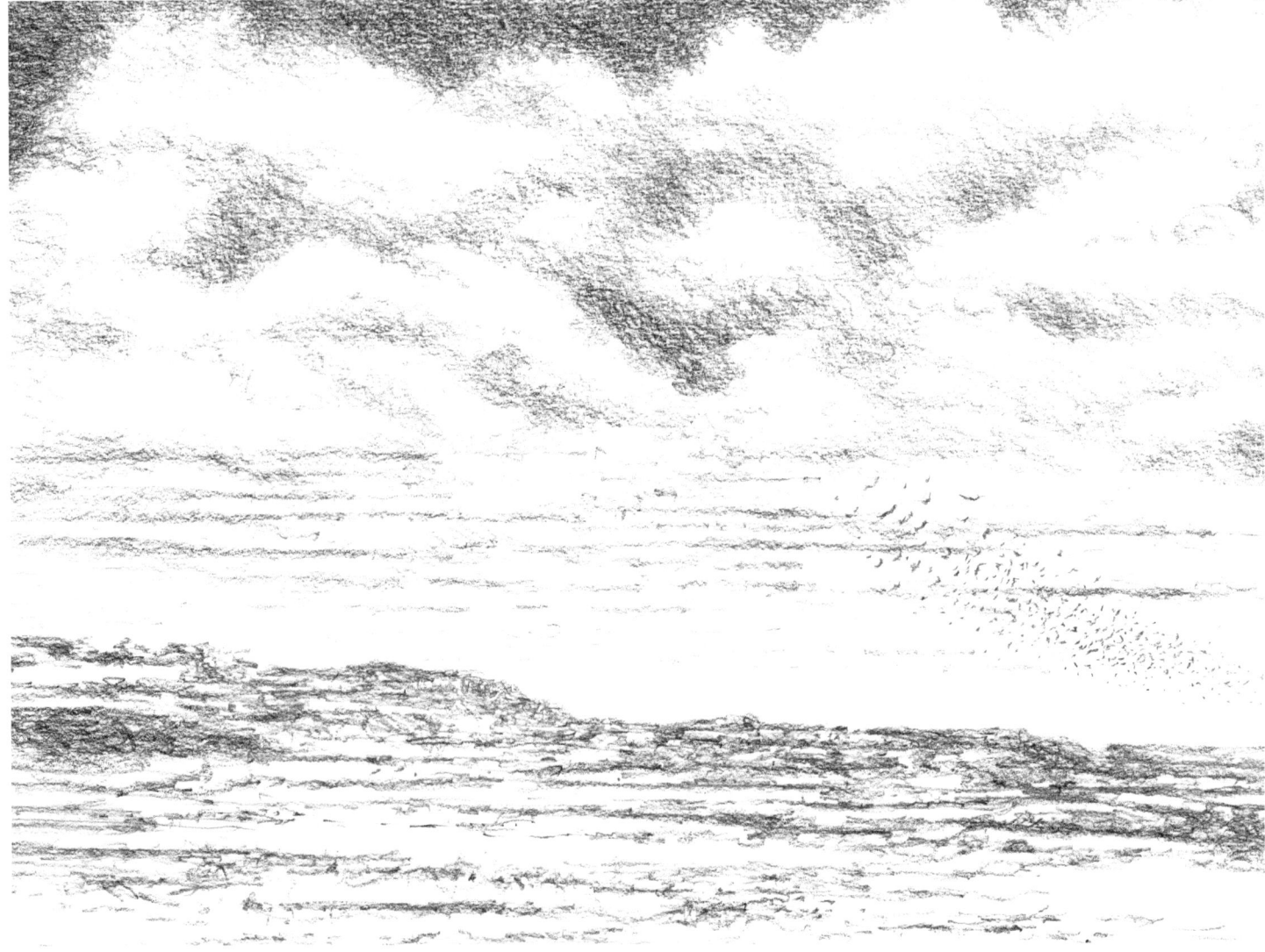

Cloud of Starlings
Pencil 290 x 420 mm

Maybe it is due to the fact that human inhabitants are minimal here that these lands are abundant with birdlife. On occasion at the end of day innumerable flocks swarm the horizon and form living clouds that can darken the sky.

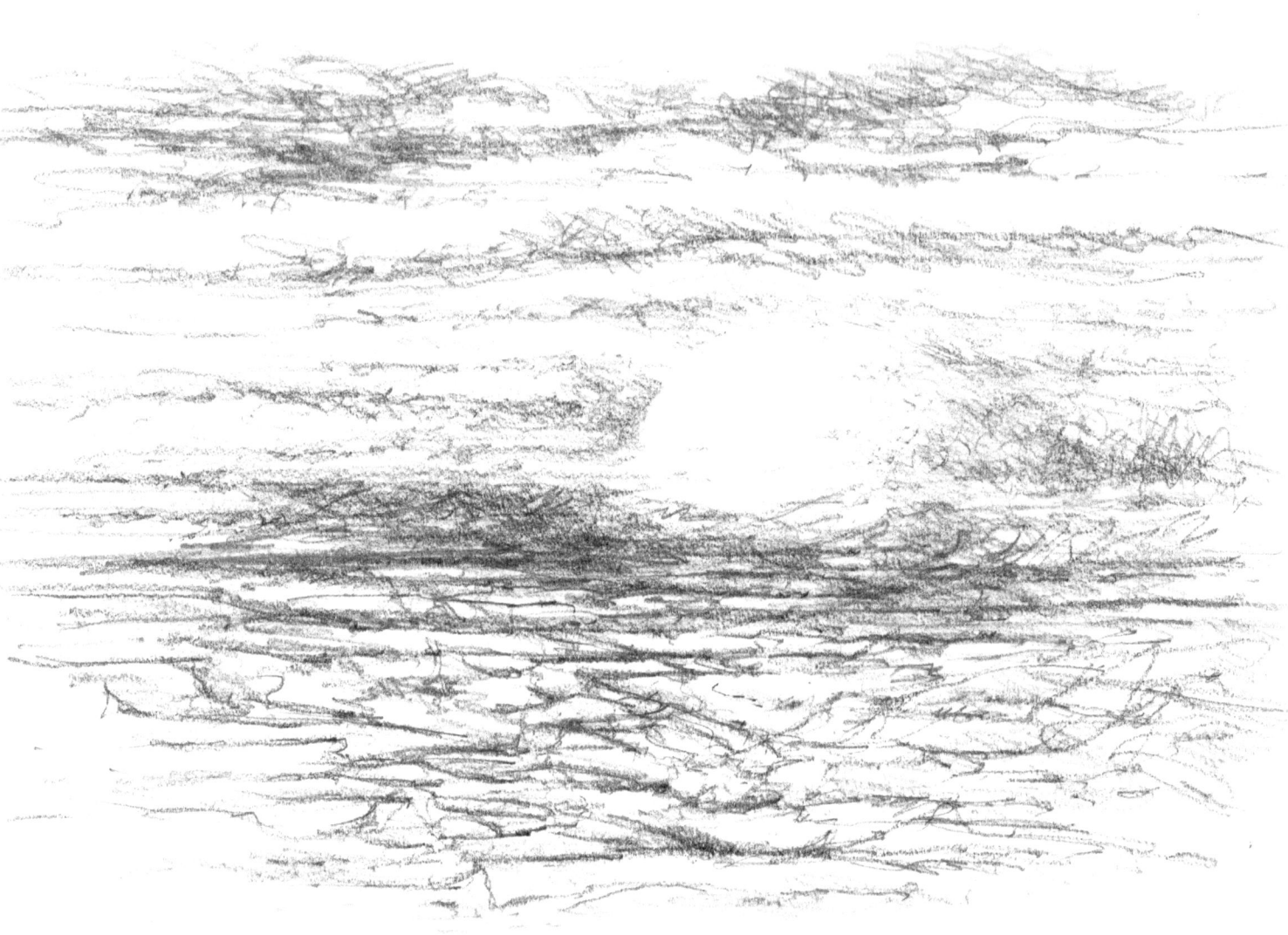

Sundown
Pencil 290 x 420 mm

Being this close to nature and the natural elements encourages thoughts that are most intriguing but are sometimes disturbing. As the sun disappears below the horizon we are as always confident that it will again rise and bring about the dawn. That will not always be the case. One day, sometime there will be no more sun and therefore no us. We should cherish the now and this blessing.

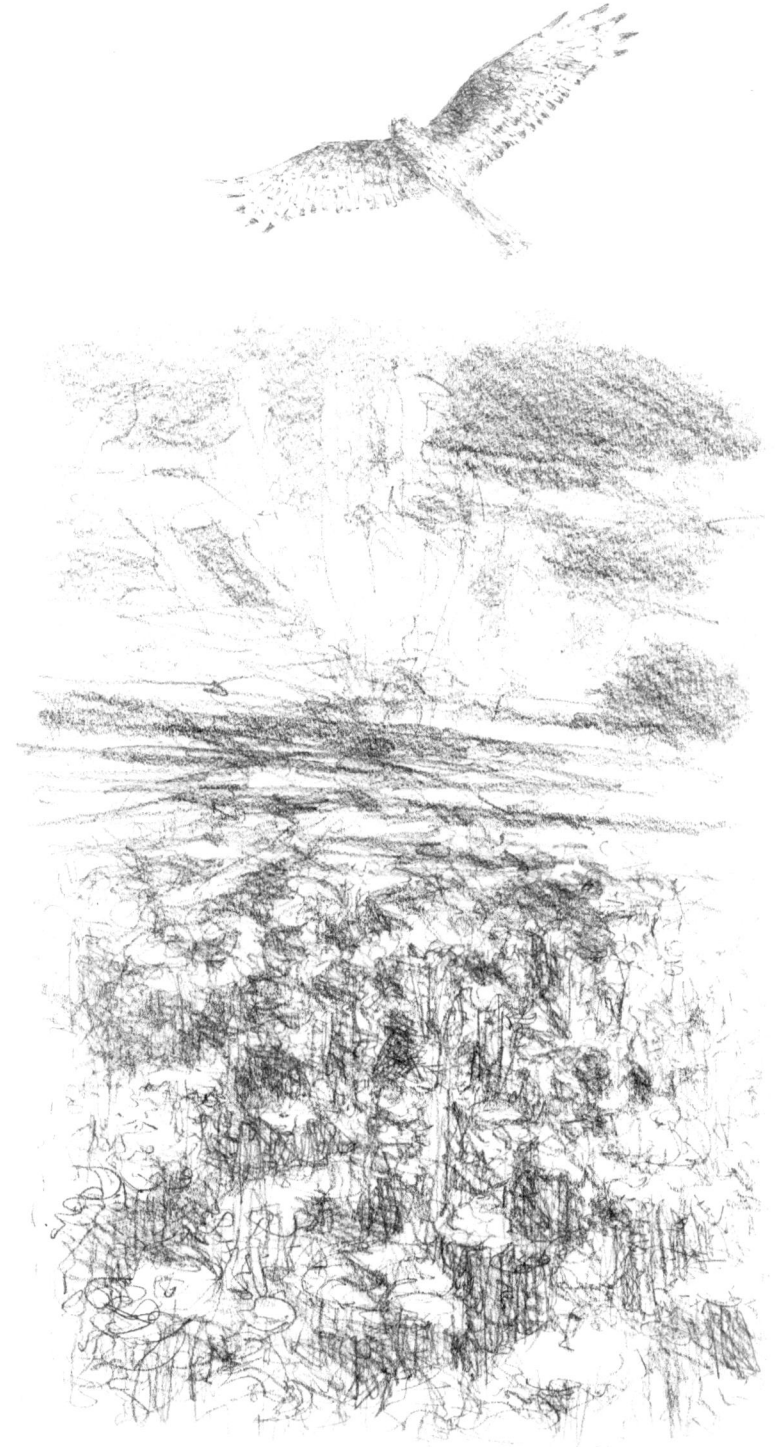

Harrier Above [Top]
Pencil 200 x 200 mm

Sunburst [Bottom]
Pencil 297 x 210 mm

In spite of any doubts or
superstitions the sun again rises
to illuminate yet another day.
The harrier glides the skies with
an eye for it's prey. Plant life rises,
twists, and turns to maximise
the benefits that it derives from
the sun's rays. Same sun,
another new day.

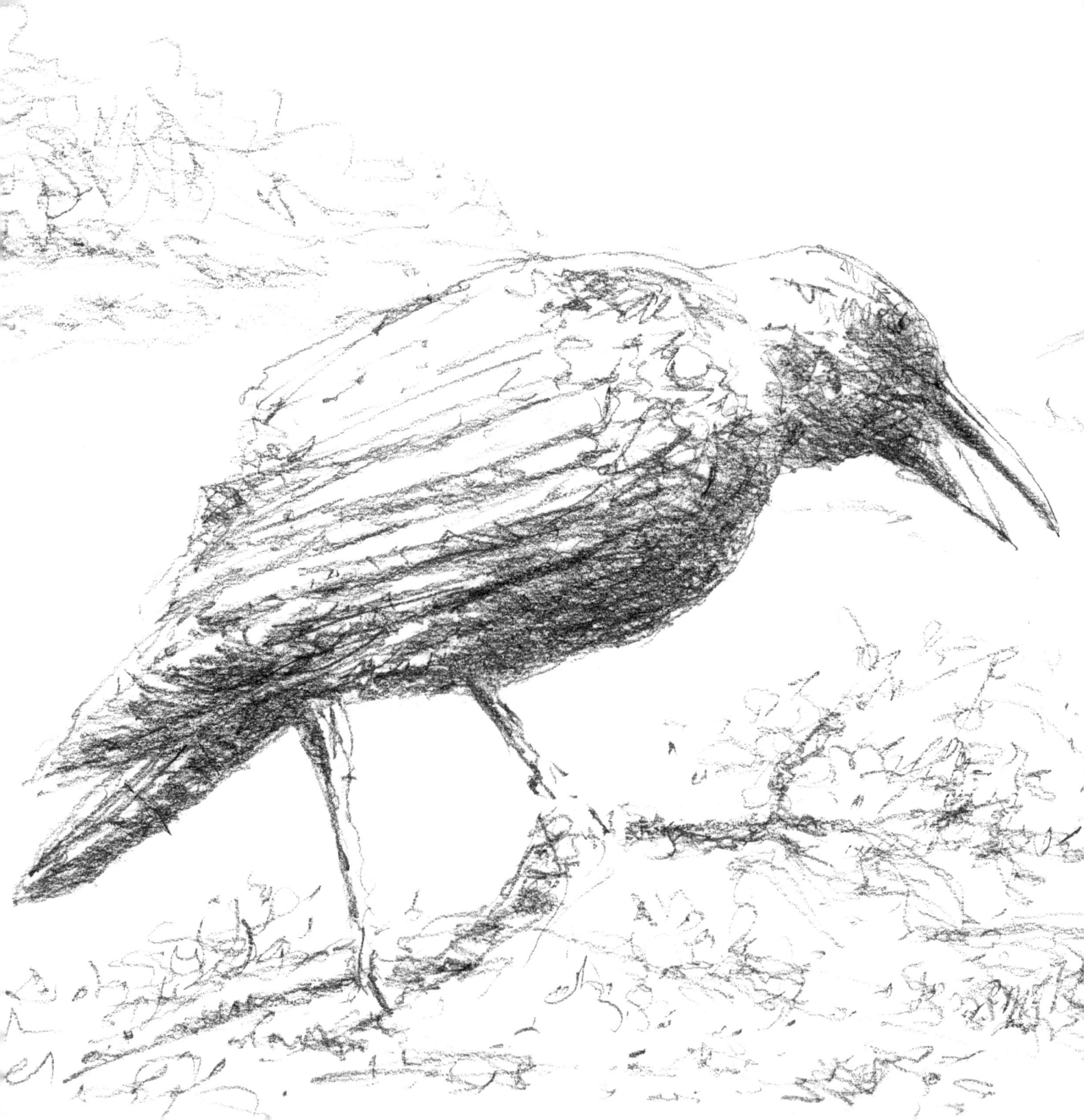

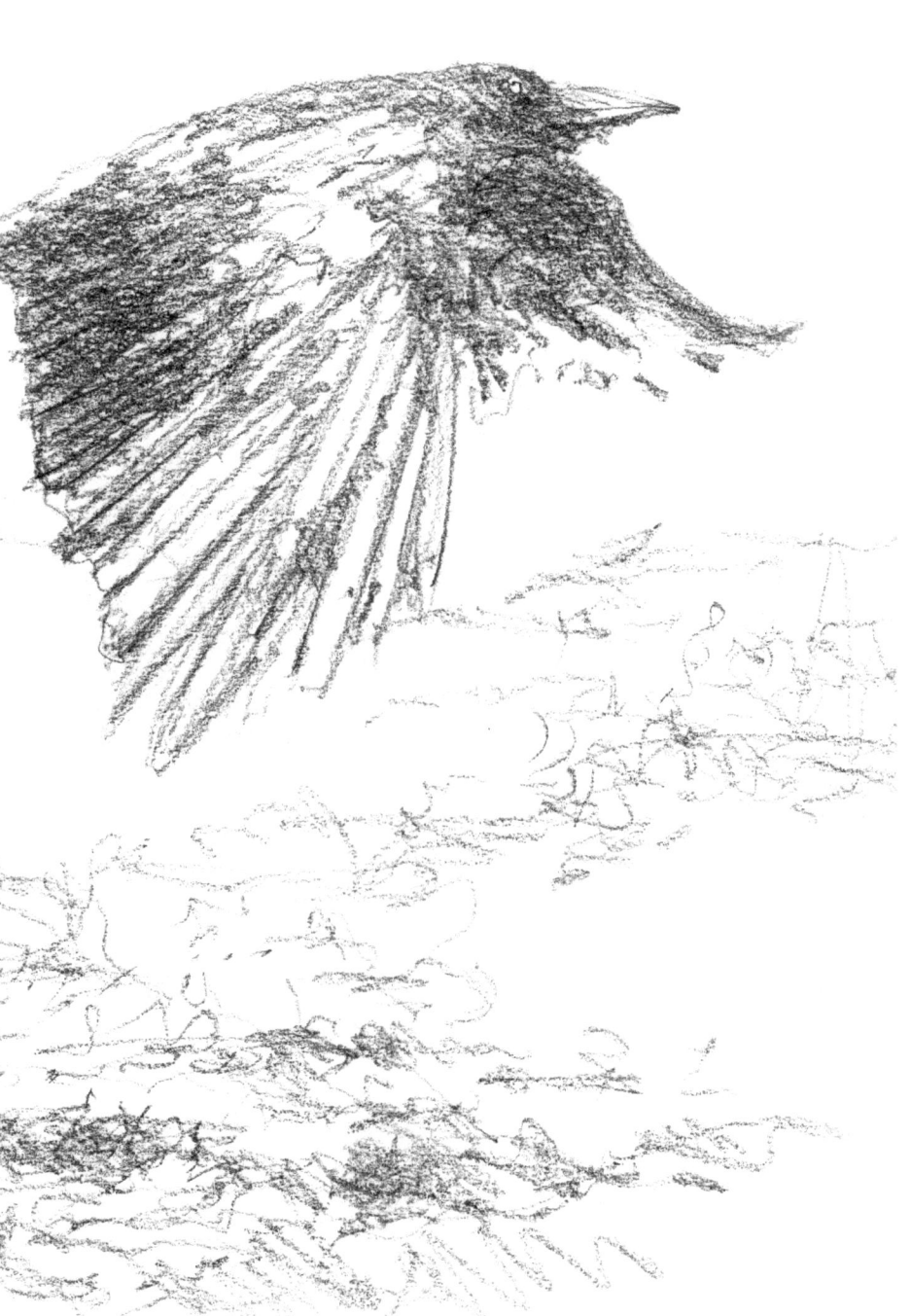

Blue Black Crows
Pencil 290 x 420 mm

Summer or winter, crows survive here perfectly well. Their blue black plumage repels the hot sunshine in summer and their sturdily built nests keep them warm during the winter months. These birds have a relatively good relationship with man. We don't bother them and they don't bother us. That's apart from their odd raids on our crops and cornfields of course, and the possibility of a shotgun encounter. The moorlands are for the crow the safest place to be.

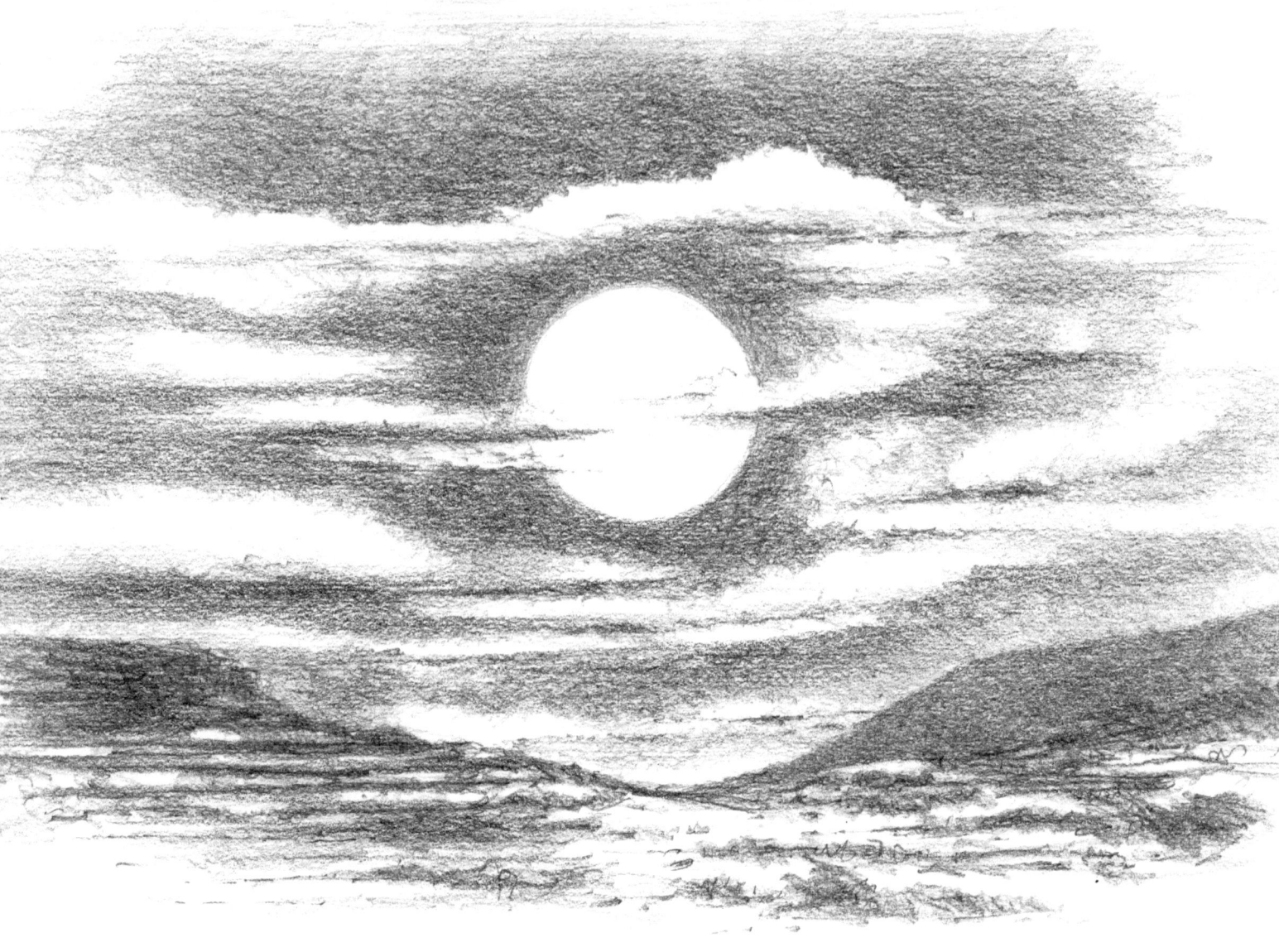

Sunset in the Valley [Page Left]
Pencil 290 x 420 mm

God's Breath [Page Right]
Pencil 290 x 420 mm

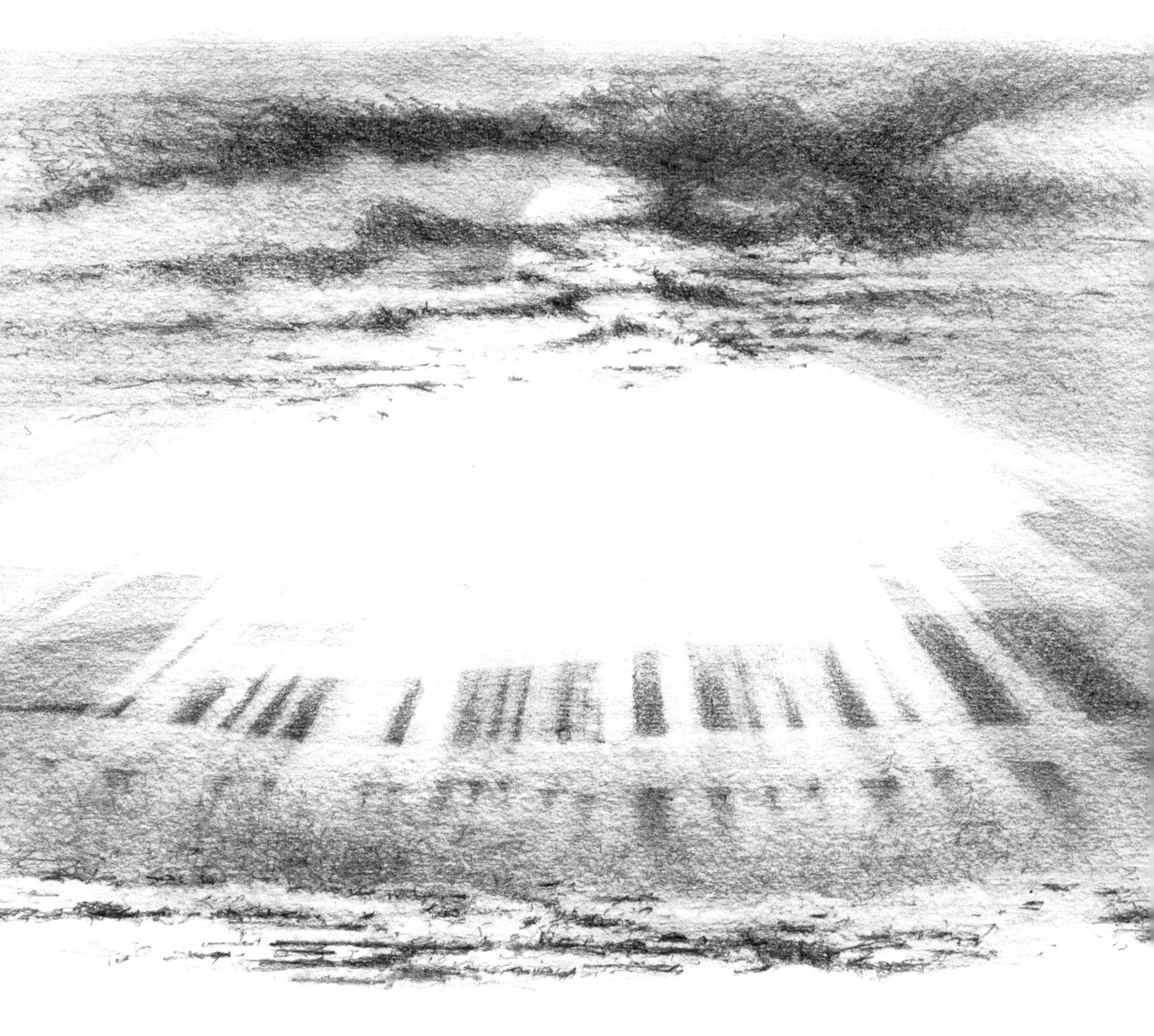

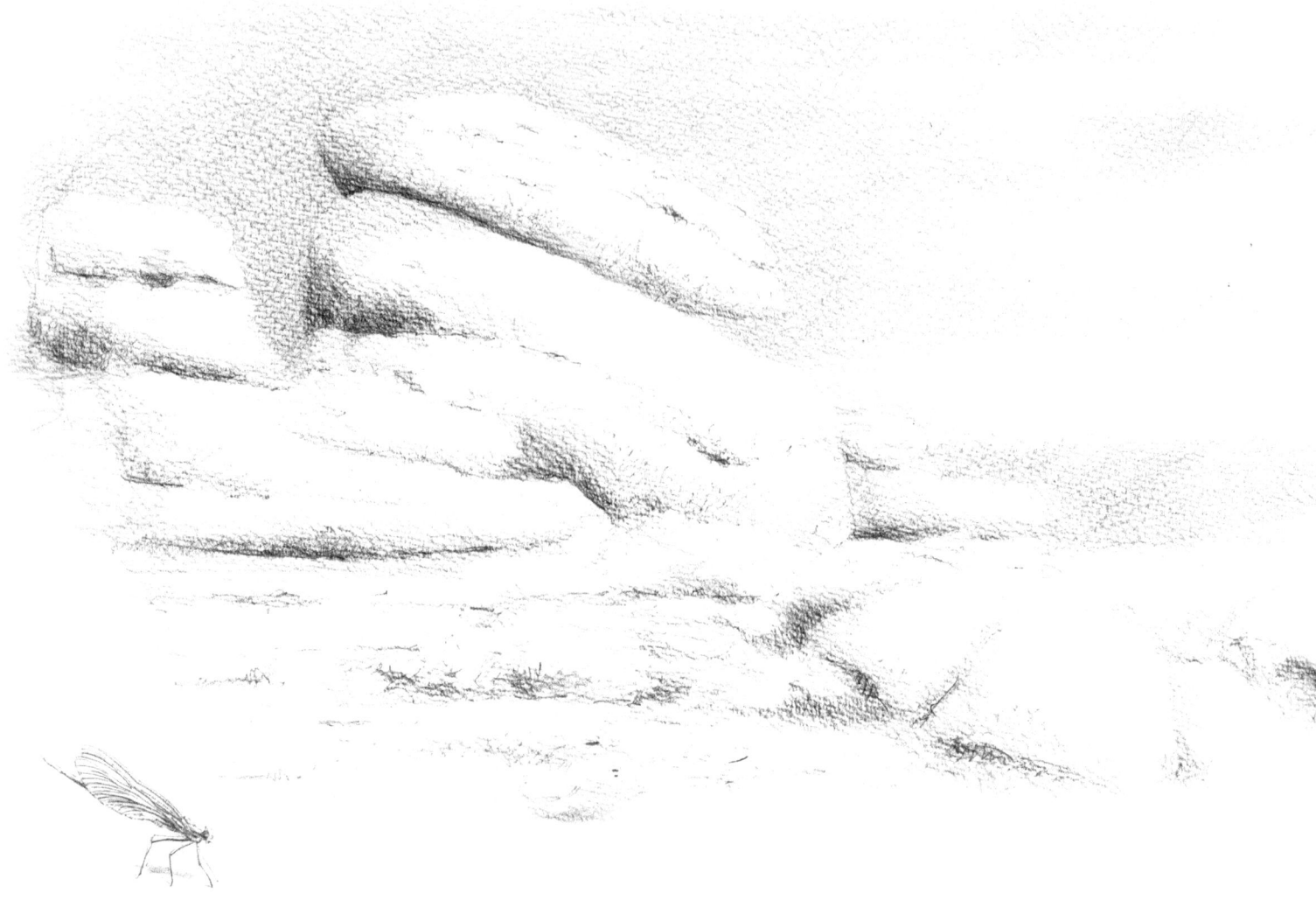

Dragonfly [Bottom Left]
Pencil 200 x 200 mm

Smiling Rocks [centre]
Pencil 290 x 420 mm

Bloodshot Sky [Page Right]
Watercolour 340 x 540 mm

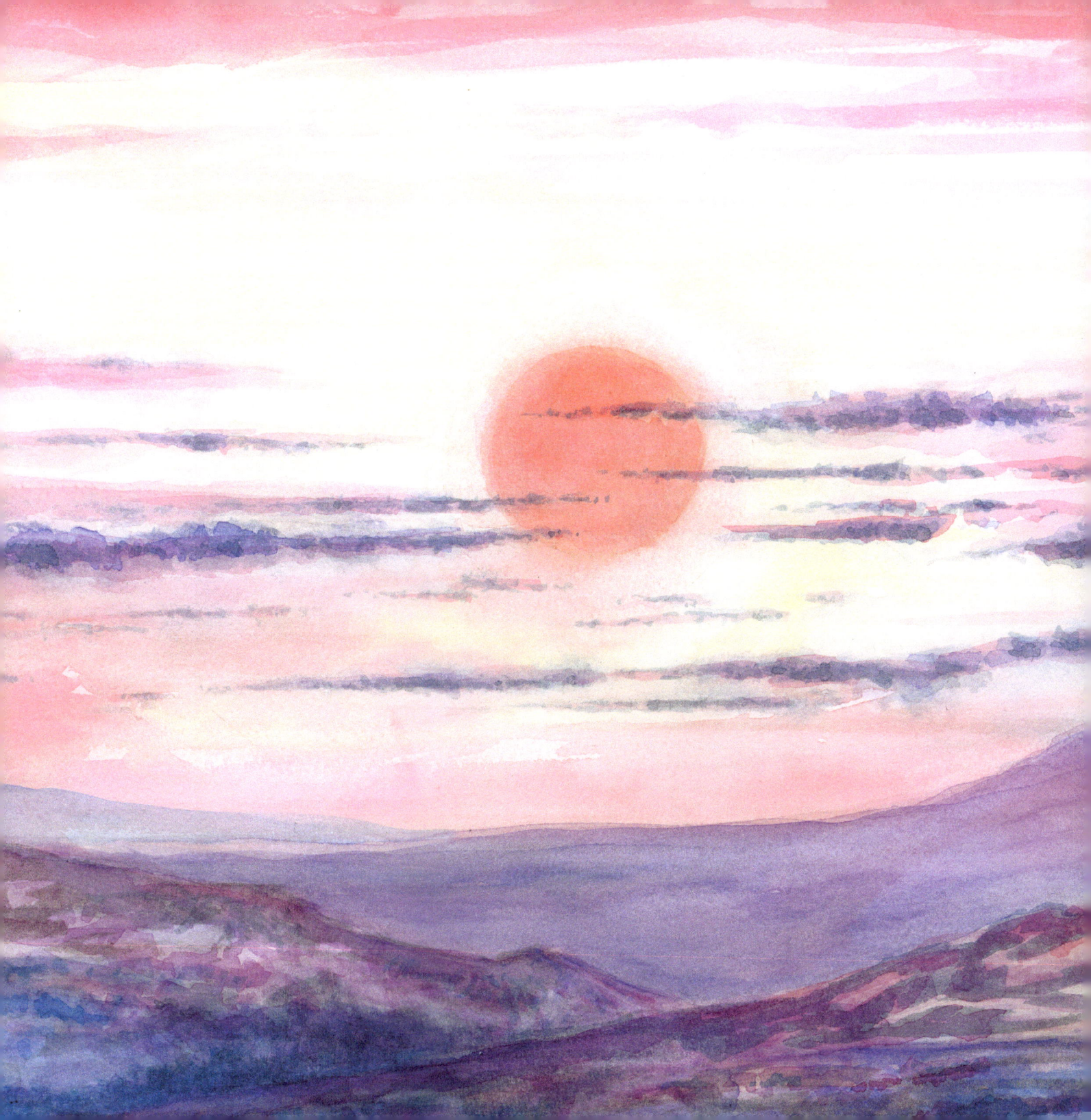

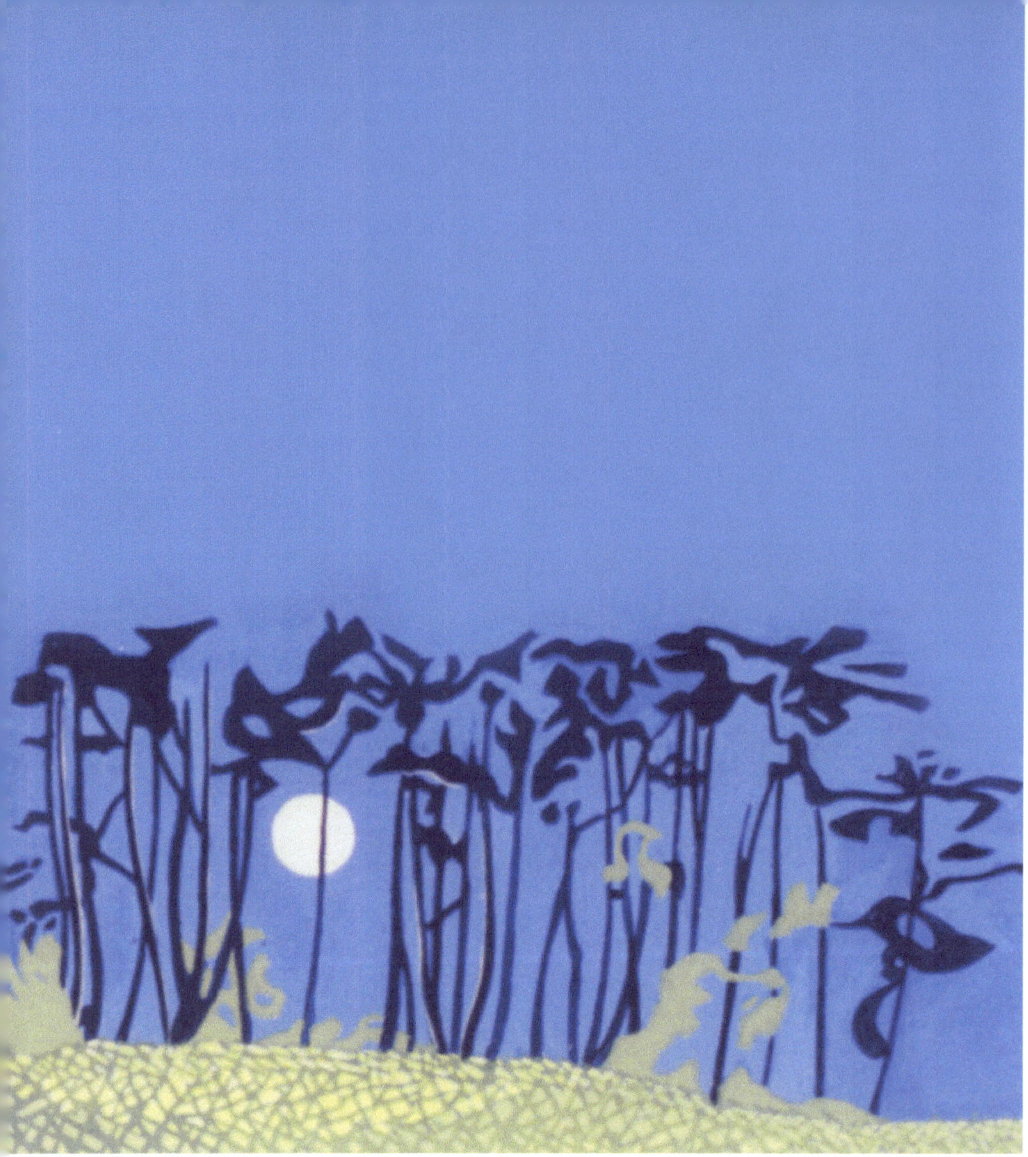

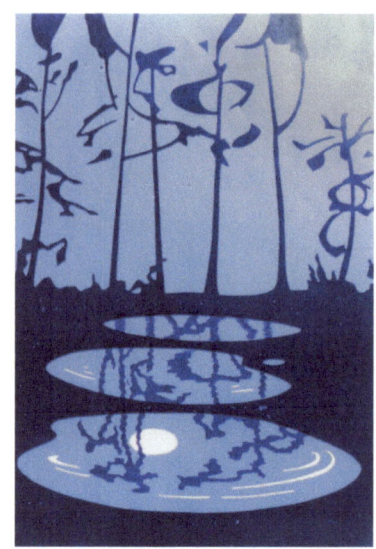

Moon in the Spinney
Linocut Print 540 x 340 mm

The Spinney
Linocut Print 340 x 340 mm

Towards the end of the long dry summer with little rainfall water becomes a precious commodity on the moorlands. The levels of rivers and reservoirs become low and some of the upland streams disappear completely. An occasional welcome shower can often be a life saving occurrence. Puddles left after the rain help sustain the wildlife here.

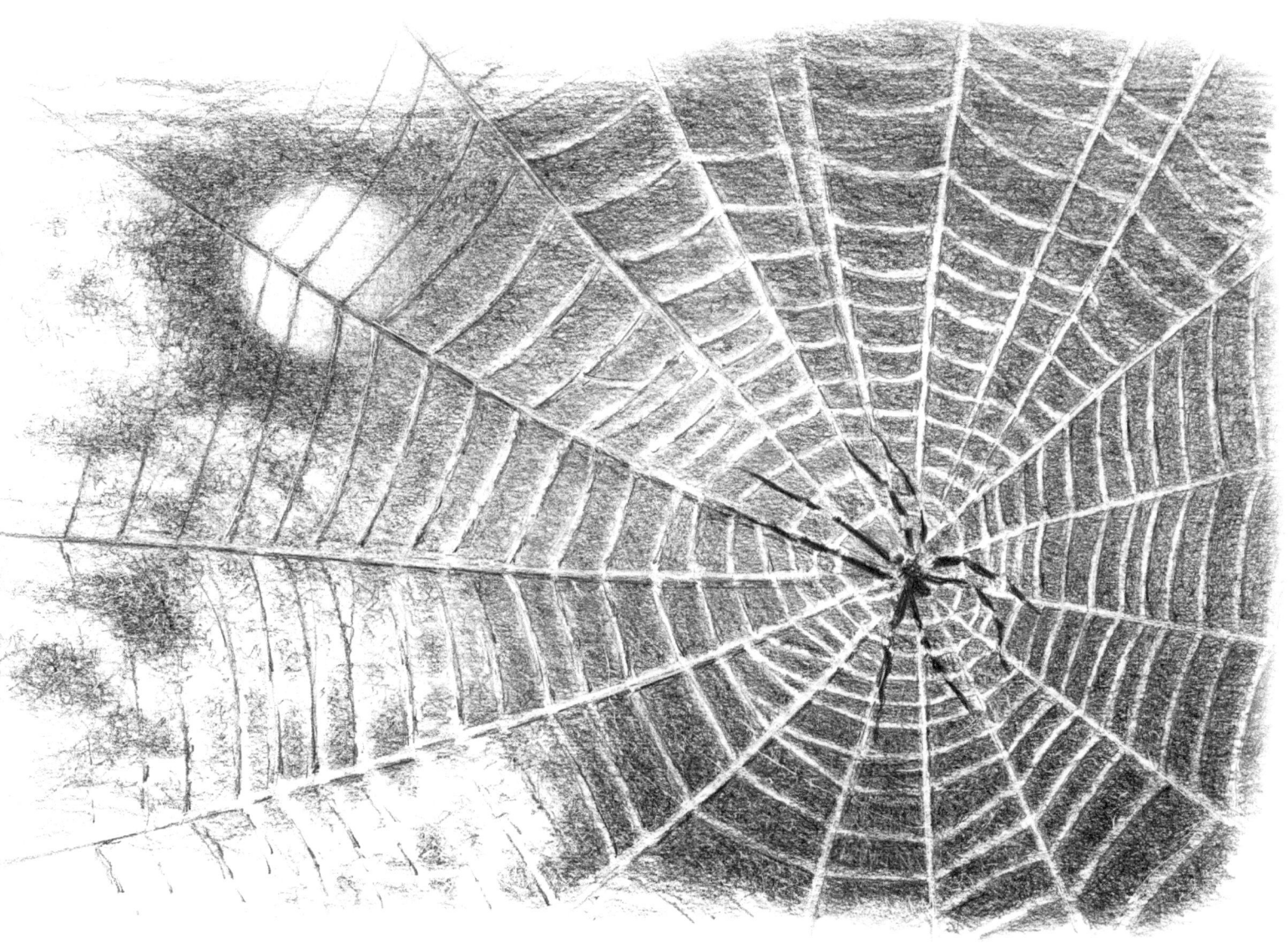

She Just Waits
Pencil 290 x 420 mm

Some predators spend most of their lives flying, swimming, or running around looking for food. Others are more canny, they set a trap and wait for their prey to come to them. During the summer months when insets are abundant on the moors these energy preserving hunters thrive.

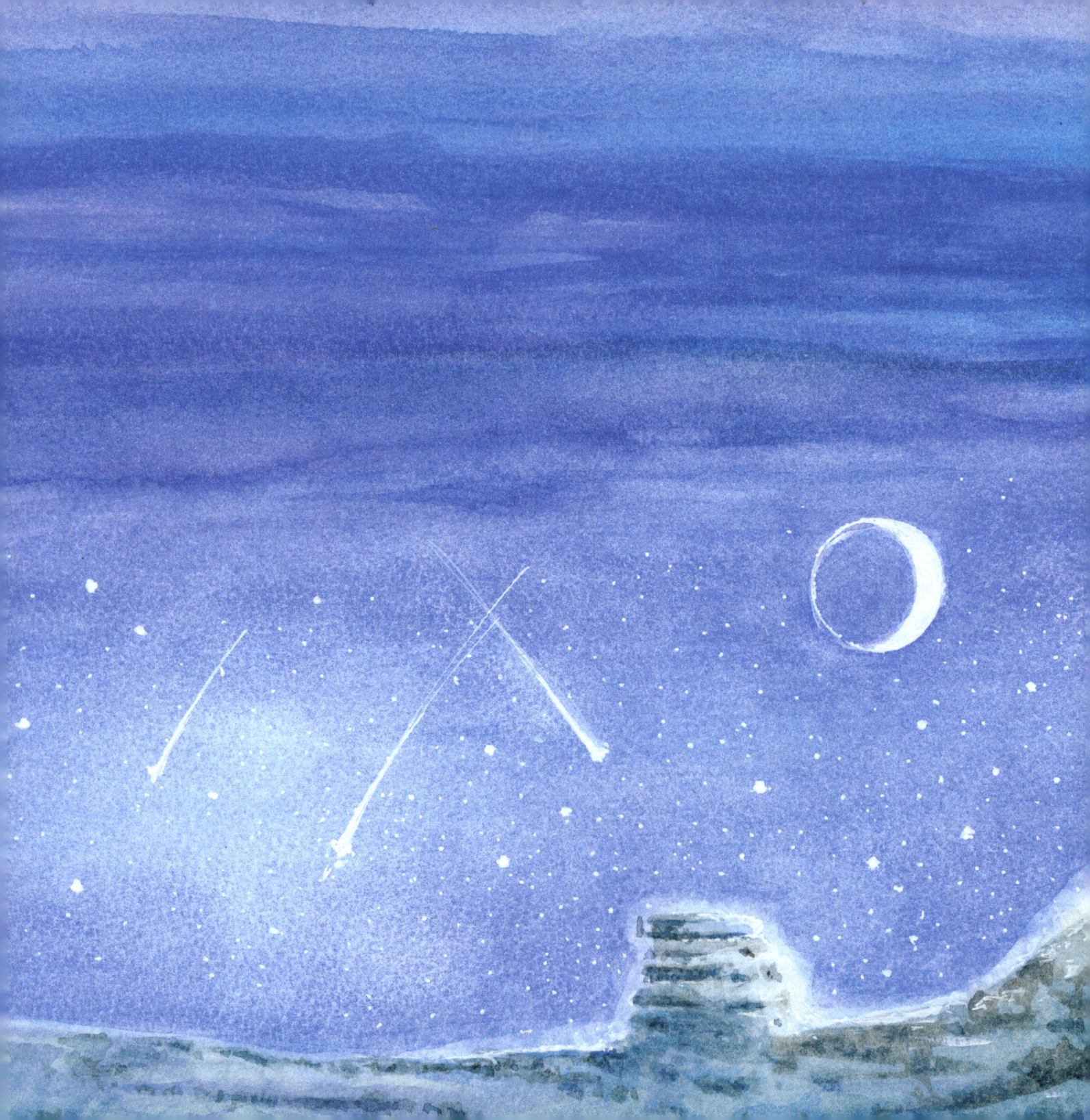

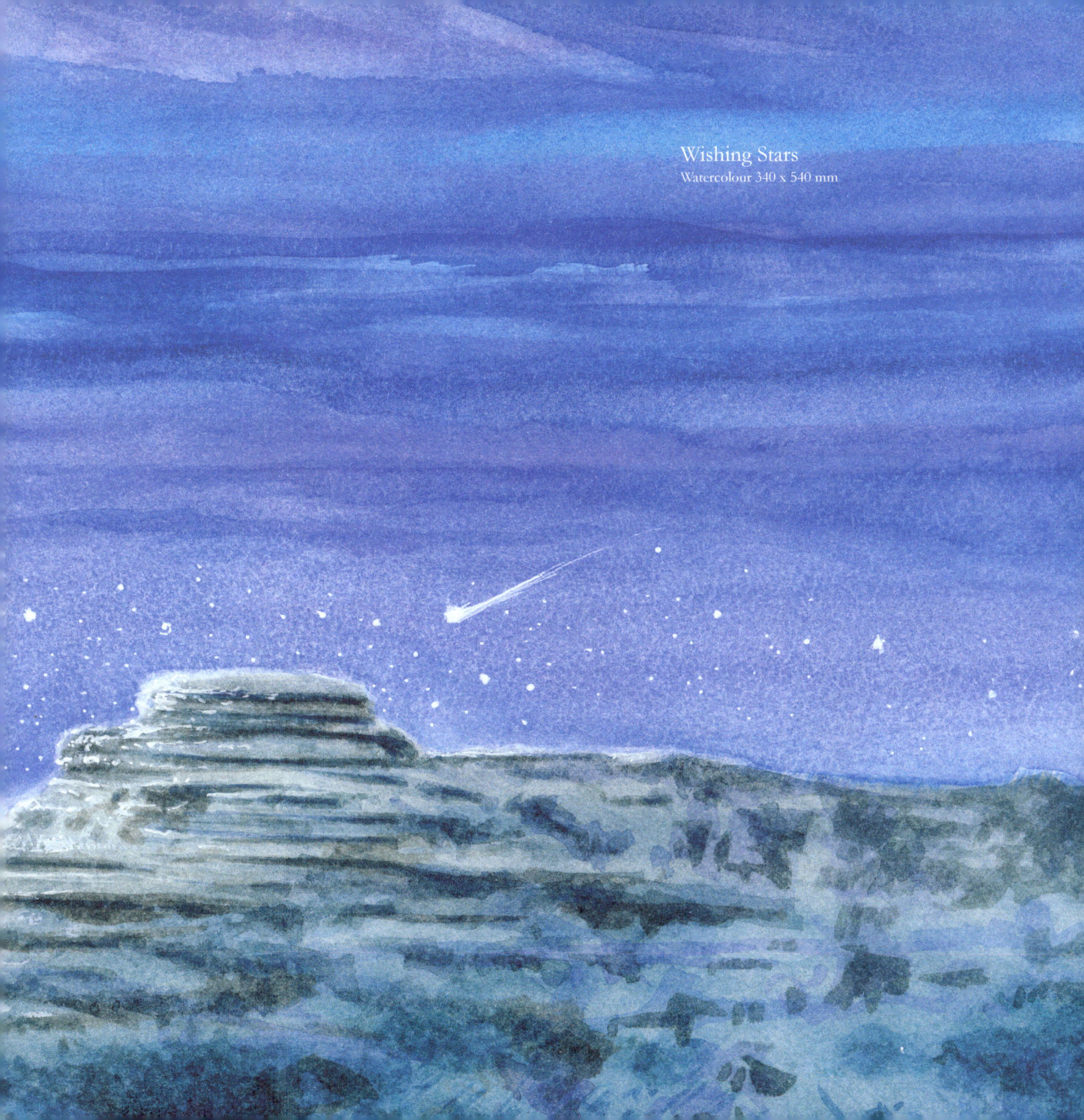

Wishing Stars
Watercolour 340 x 540 mm

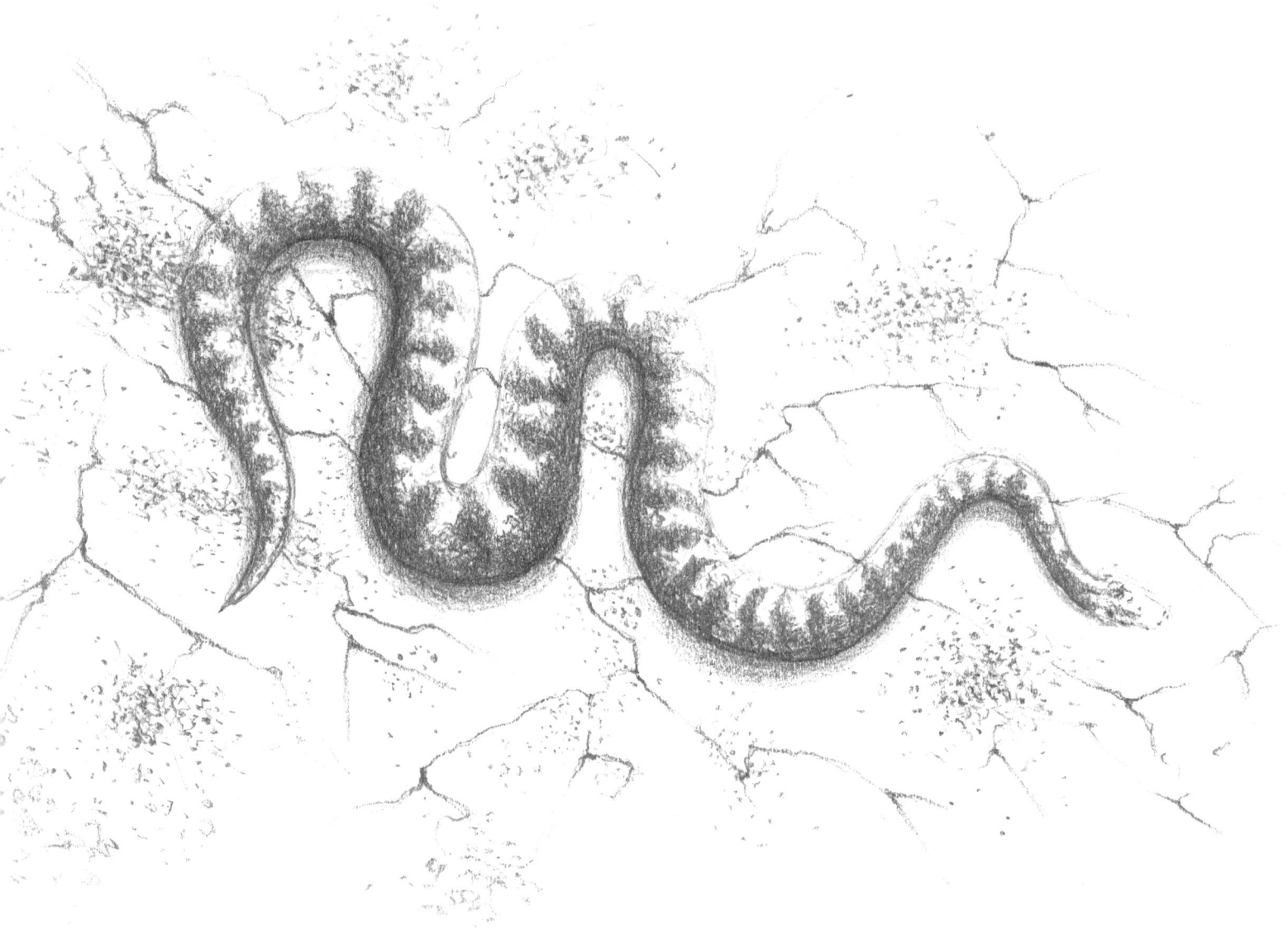

Sun Basking Adder [Page Left]
Pencil 210 x 297 mm

High Summer on the Moor [Page Right]]
Pencil 297 x 210 mm

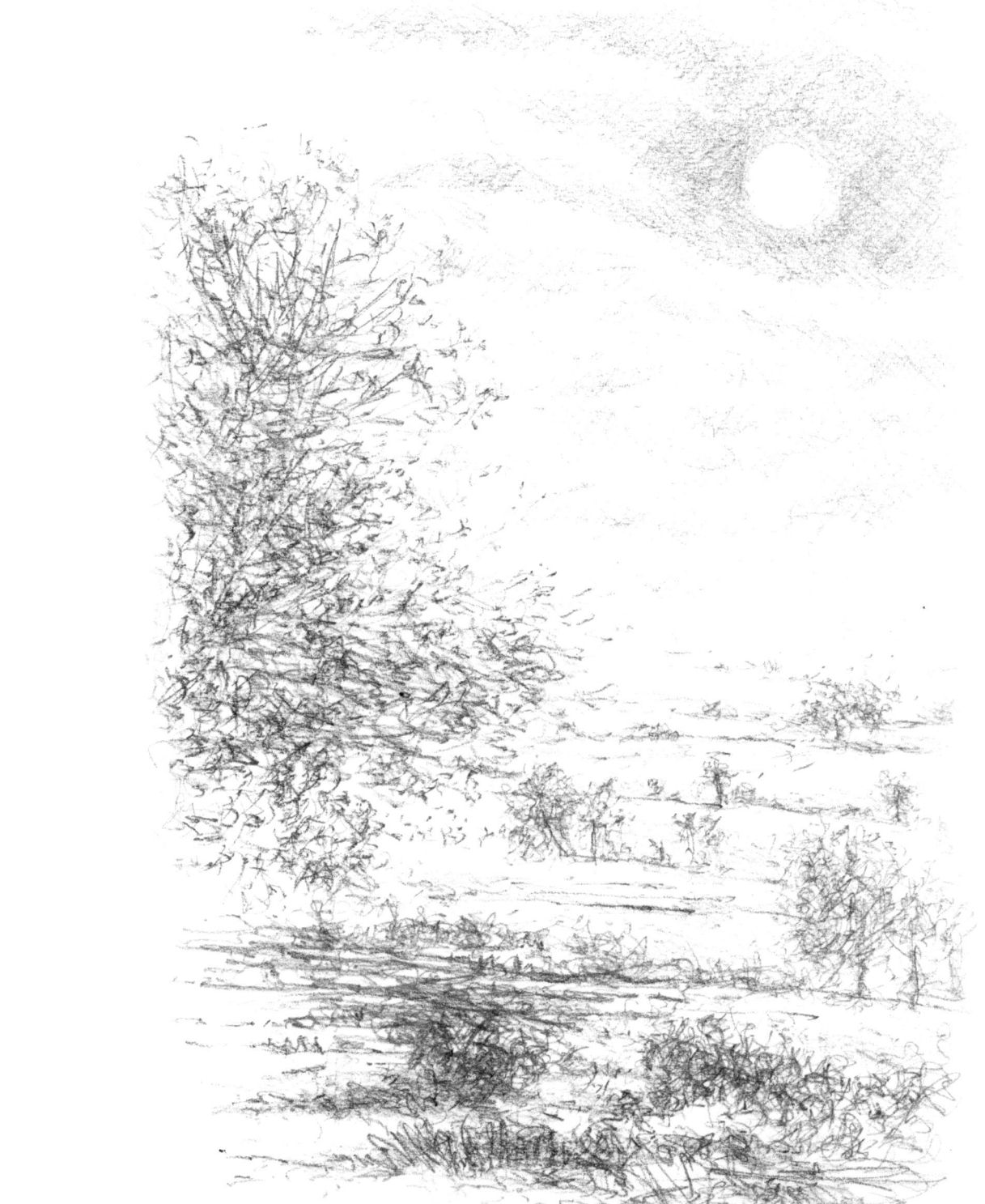

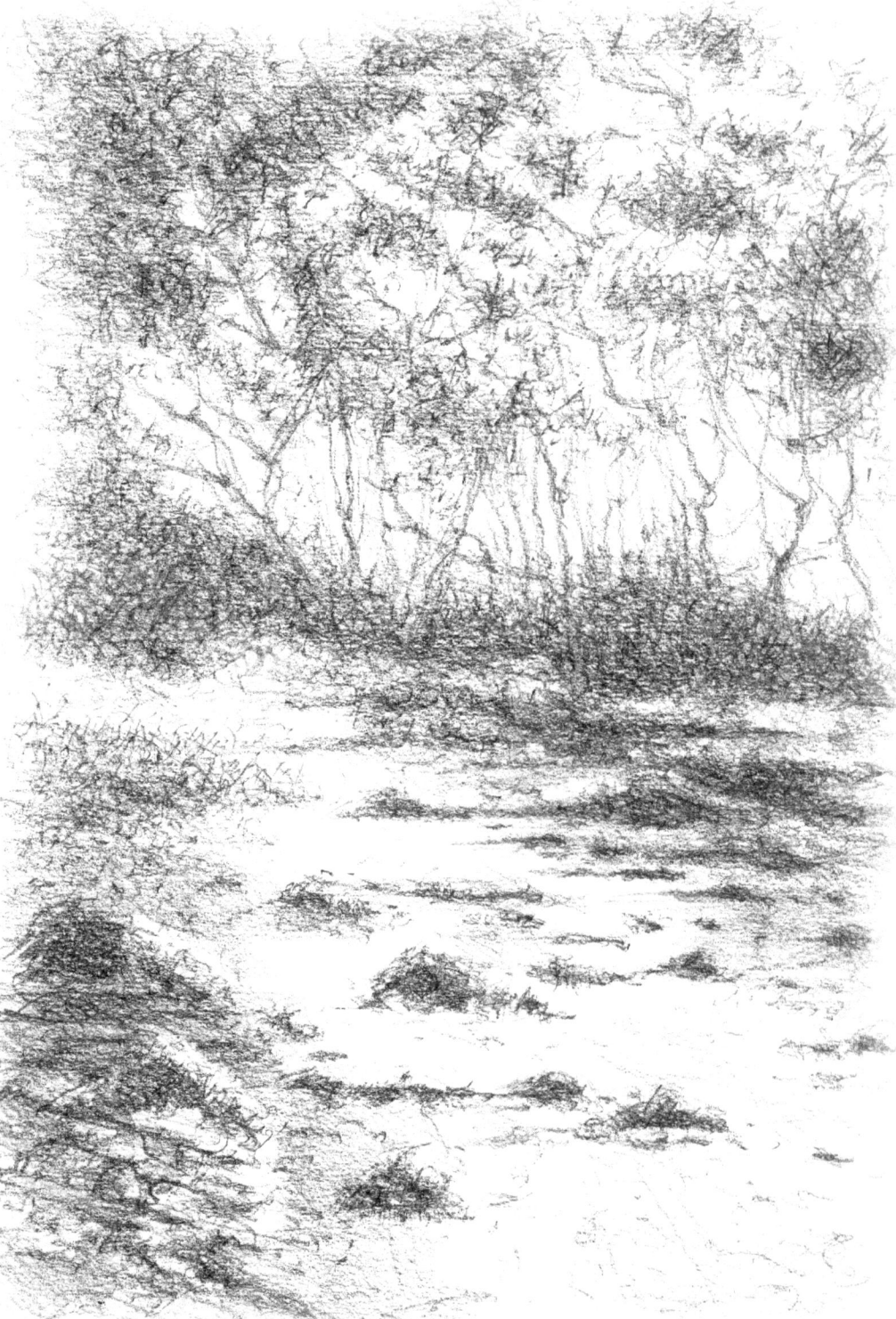

West Dart [Page Left]
Pencil 297 x 210 mm

As the days become shorter
the end of summer is
signalled. The creatures that
hibernate during the cold
months begin to prepare for
the winter. Food is consumed
in abundance and as much
body fat as possible is gained.
Nuts are stored and burrows
lined with fresh insulation.
But summer is not yet done
so some wildlife still soak up
the life giving rays of the sun.

Sunbathing Lizard [Page Right]
Pencil 210 x 297 mm

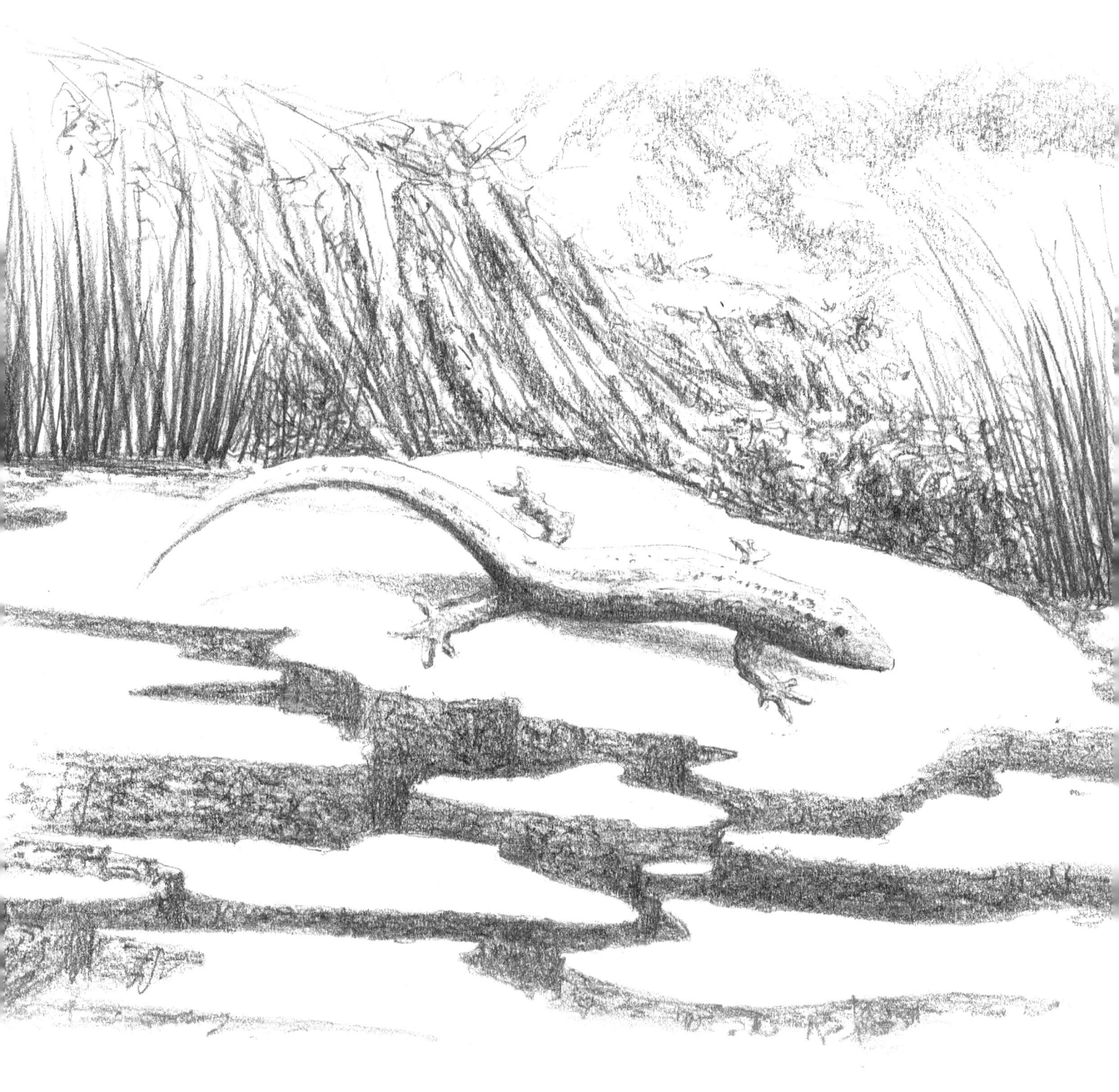

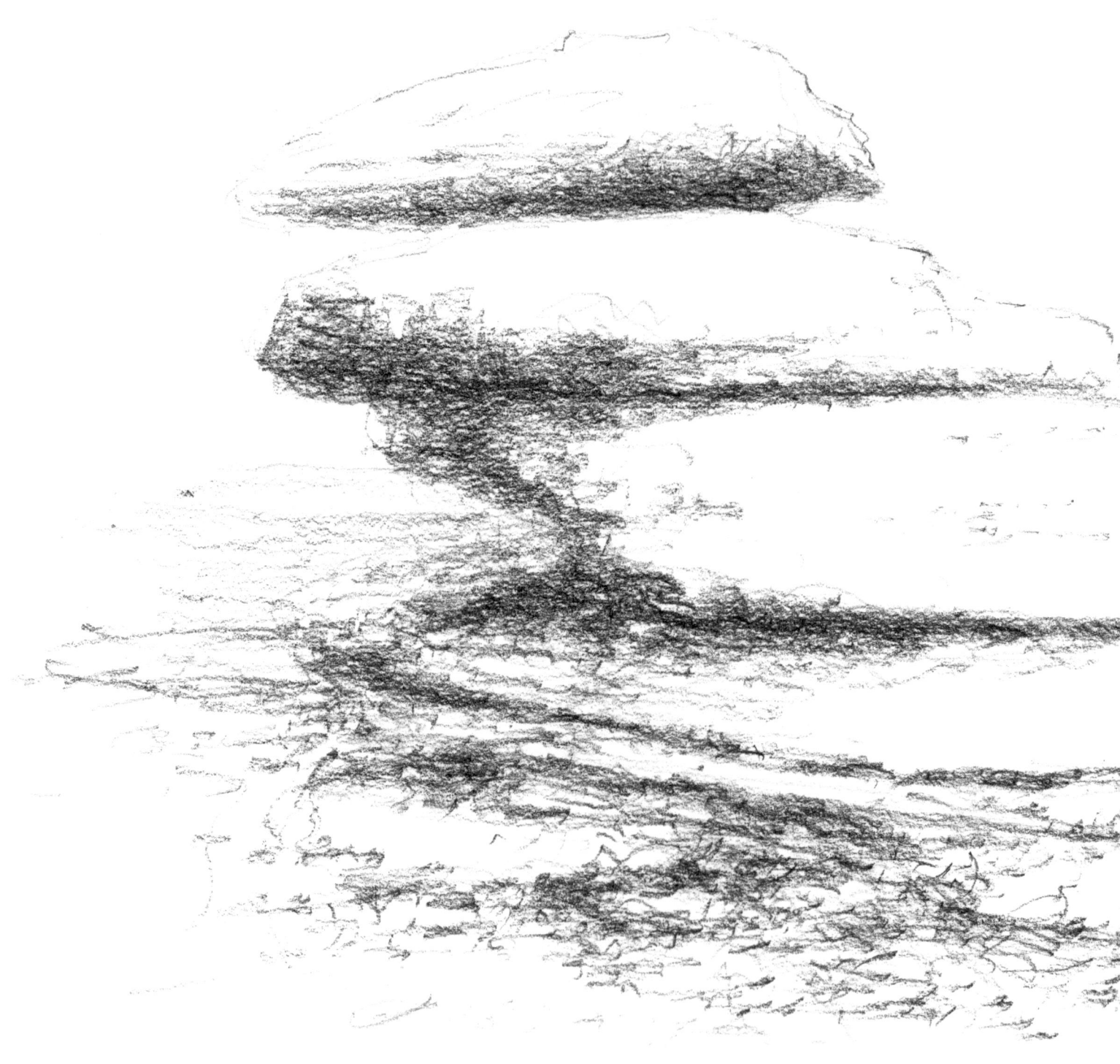

Laid-Back Rocks
Pencil 290 x 420 mm

Even the Tors seem to know that the last days of summer are close. They to may be preparing for the isolation of winter. The hawk also is aware that although food is still readily found, all too soon this will change.

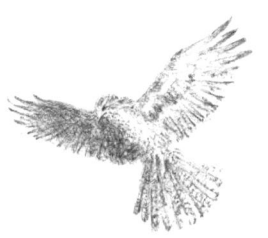

Red Tailed Hawk
Pencil 200 x 200 mm

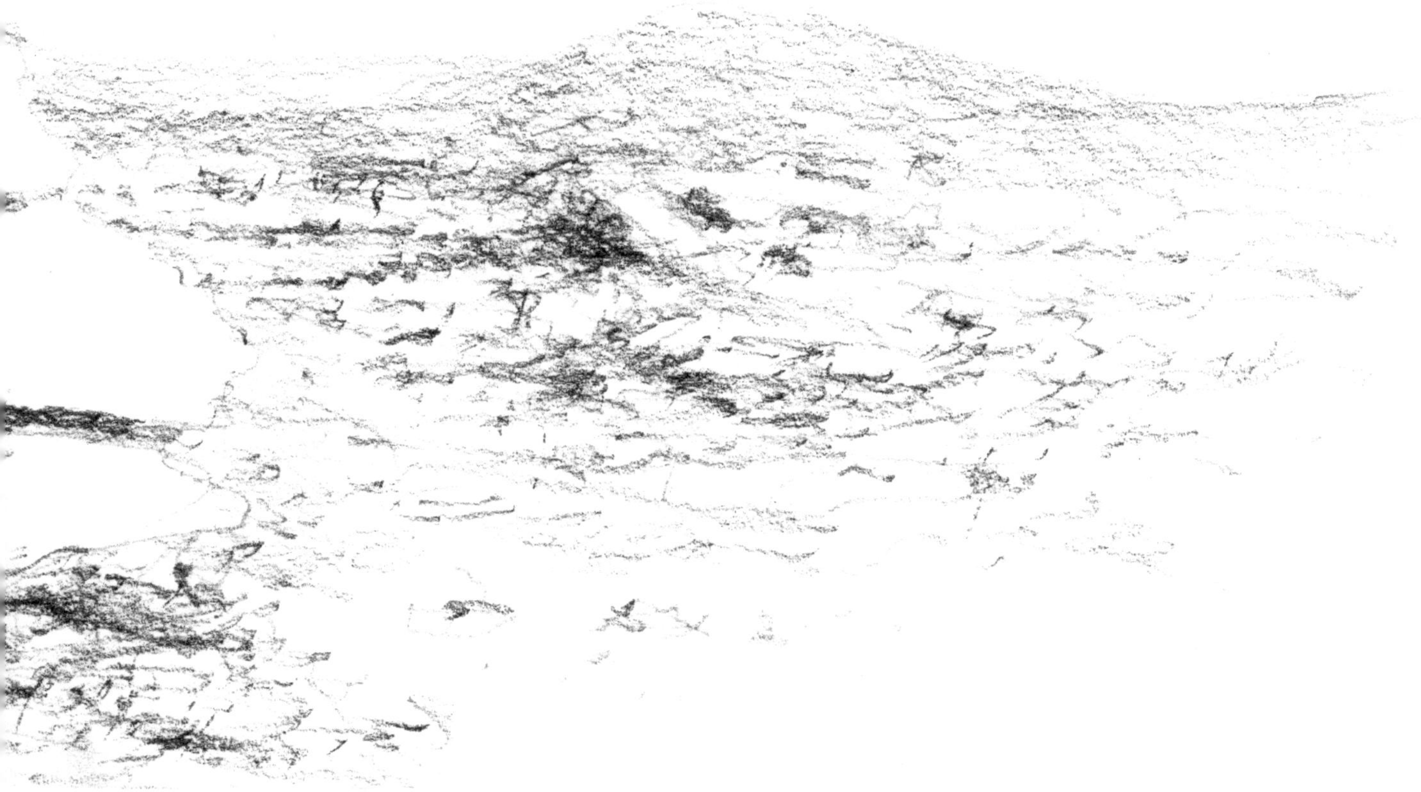

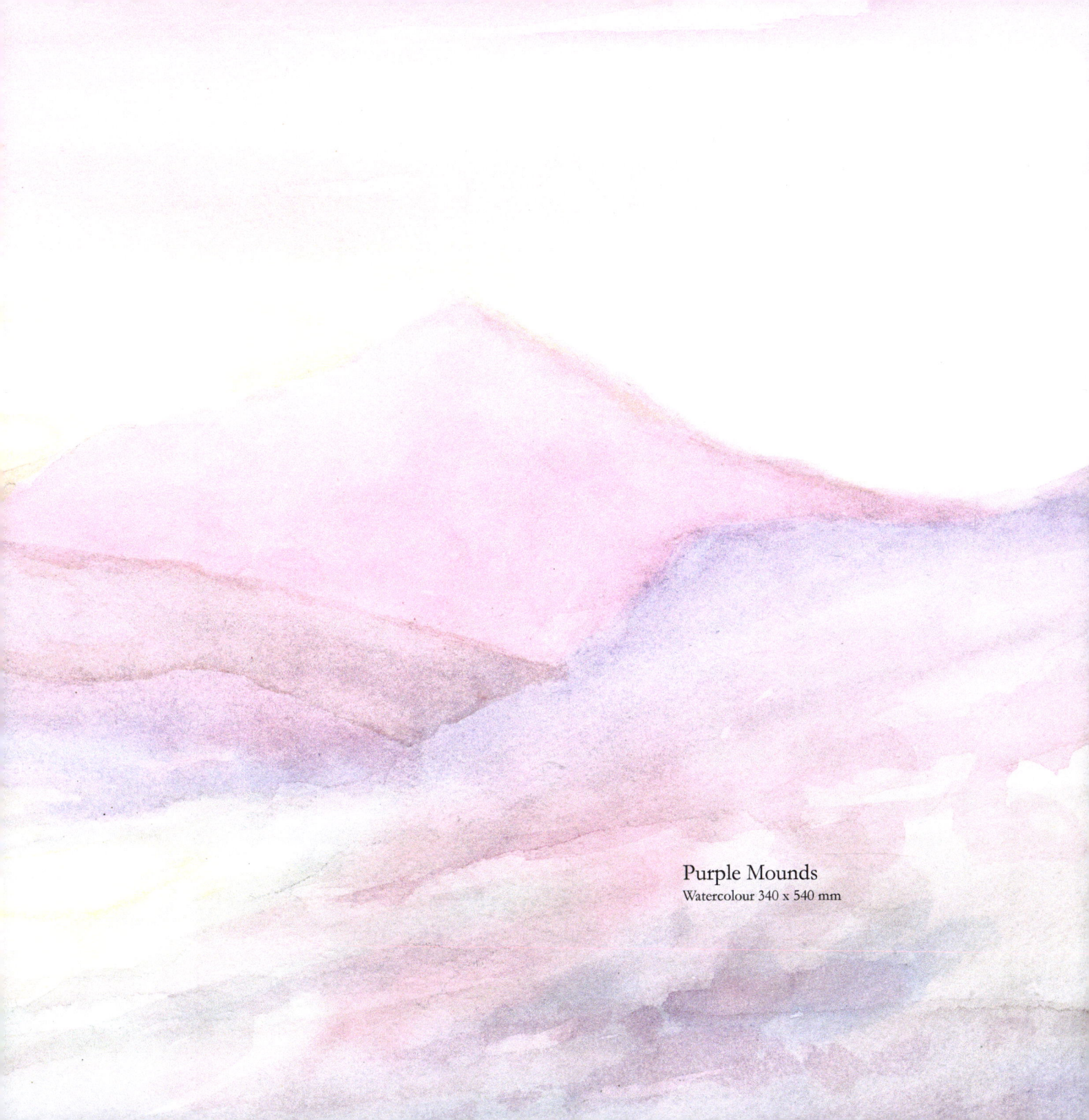

Purple Mounds
Watercolour 340 x 540 mm

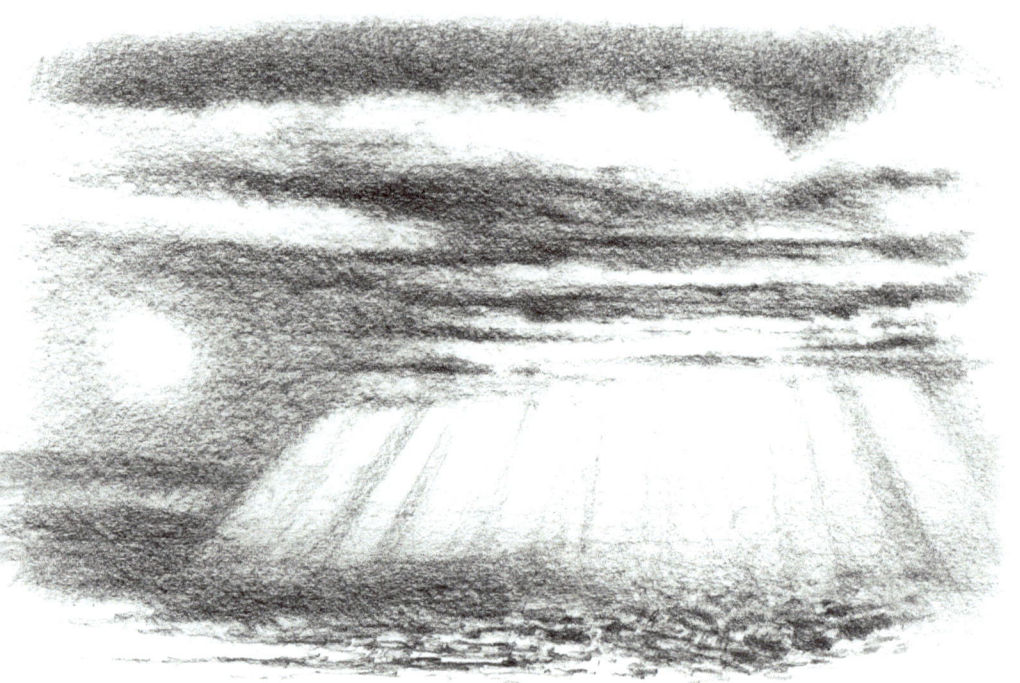

Two Gods
Pencil 210 x 297 mm

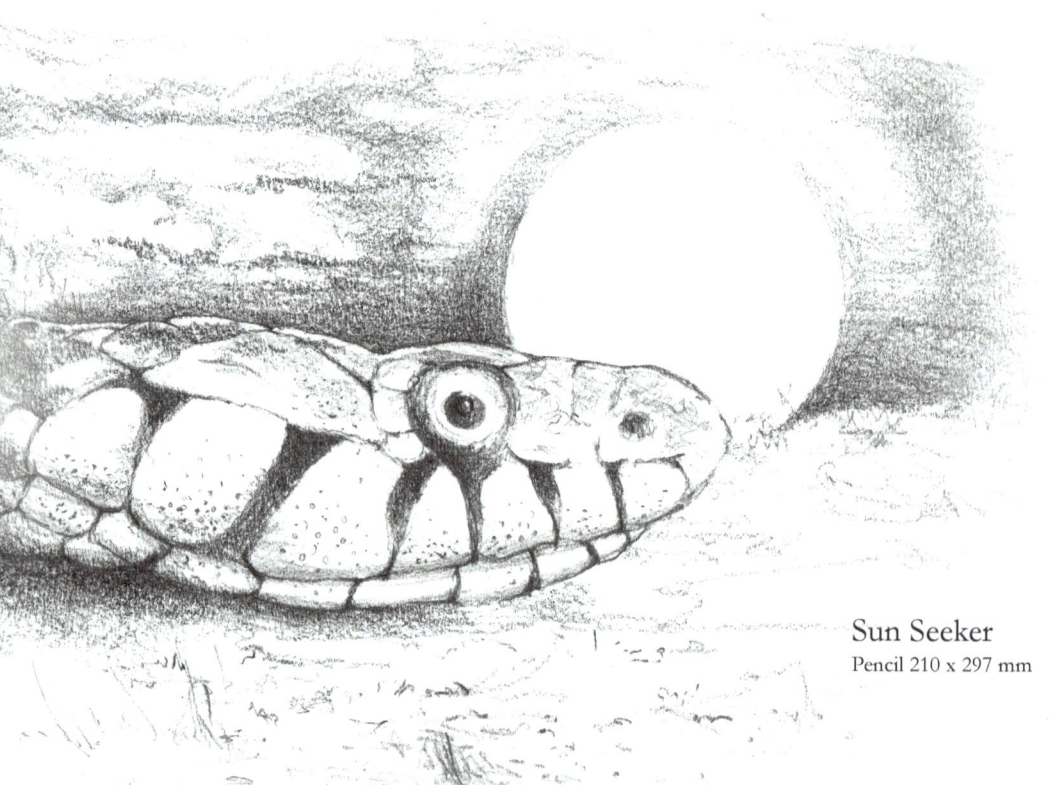

Sun Seeker
Pencil 210 x 297 mm

Last Days of Summer
Watercolour 340 x 540 mm

The air temperature begins to cool but at midday the rays of the sun can still be intense. Living things go about absorbing precious sunshine while it is still available. The land now welcomes the more frequent and much needed rainfall.

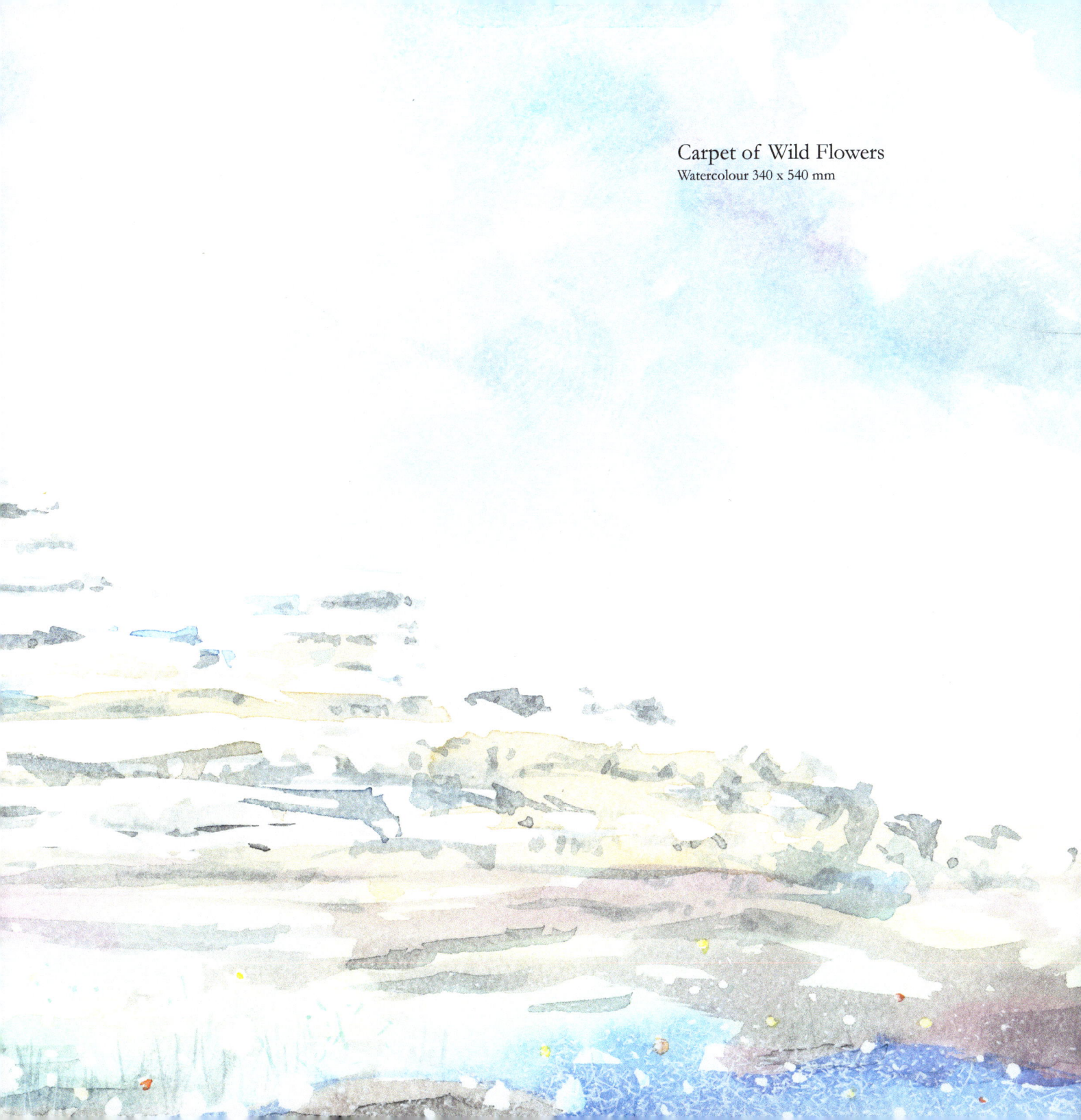

Carpet of Wild Flowers
Watercolour 340 x 540 mm

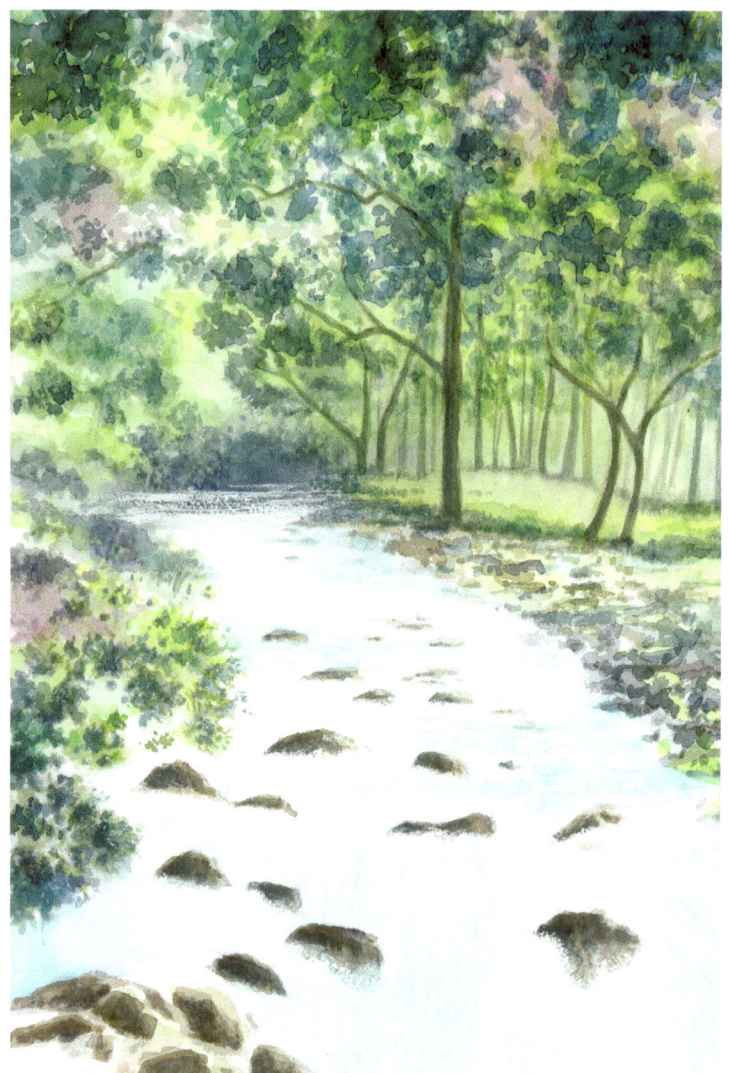

Anadromous Successful
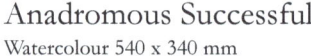
Watercolour 540 x 340 mm

Early autumn, and the rains have swollen the rivers. Water from the high hills has found it's way to the upland streams. It is again that time of year when the salmon run begins. After as much as four years since they left here, these fish return from the ocean. They fight their way upstream going from salt water to fresh where they will then produce the next generation of their kind.

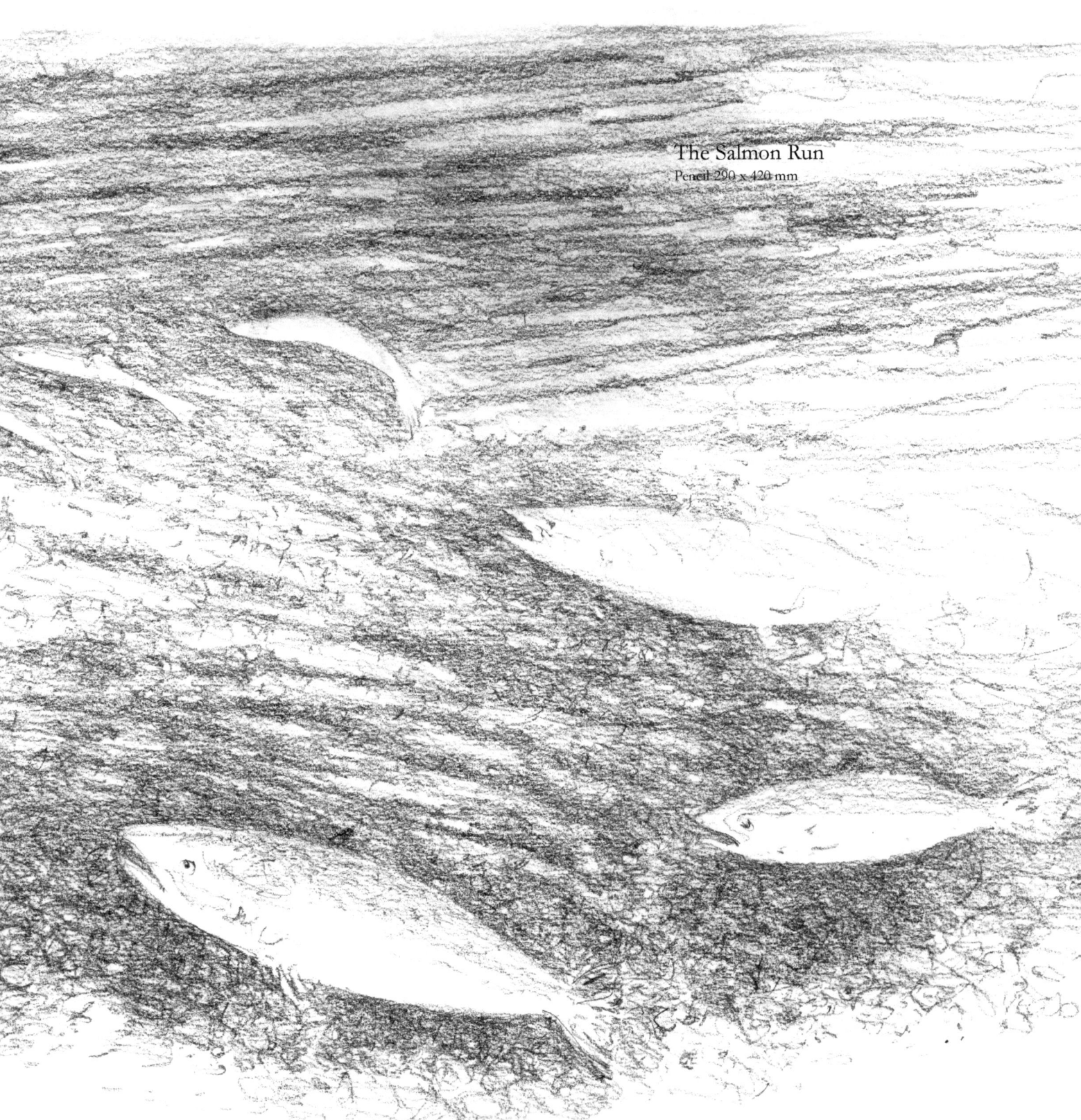

The Salmon Run
Pencil 290 x 420 mm

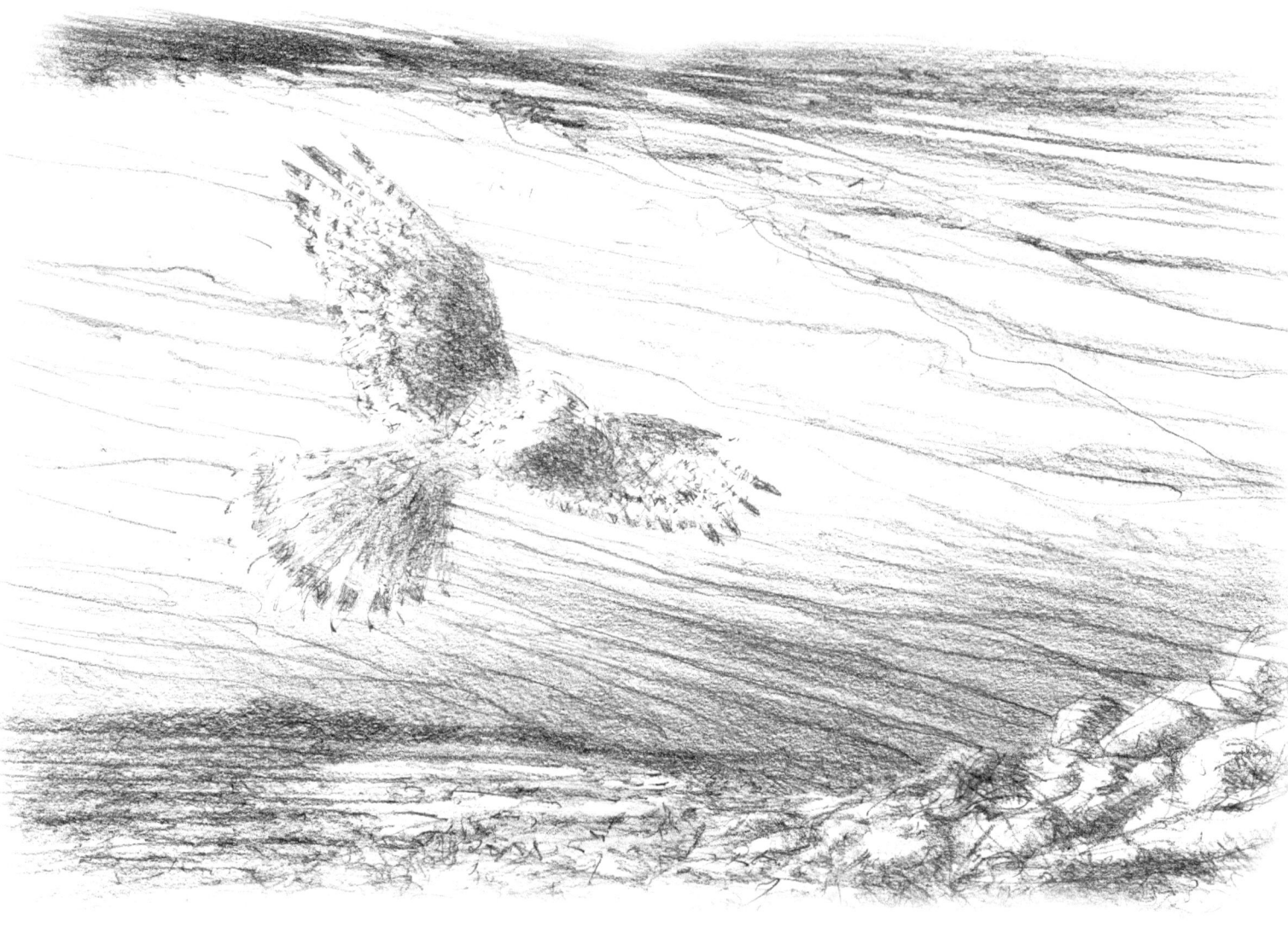

Looking for Lunch
Pencil 290 x 420 mm

Food is now much harder to find and those who are not fully fit will not survive the coming winter months. The kestrel now finds it more difficult to hunt, small rodents and insects are becoming scarce.

Old Wings
Pencil 290 x 420 mm

The snows will again soon fall. The cycle is almost complete. The sun and earth gave life and will inevitably take it away. The old must make way for the new. This is how things are and also how they should and must be. It is what we call life.

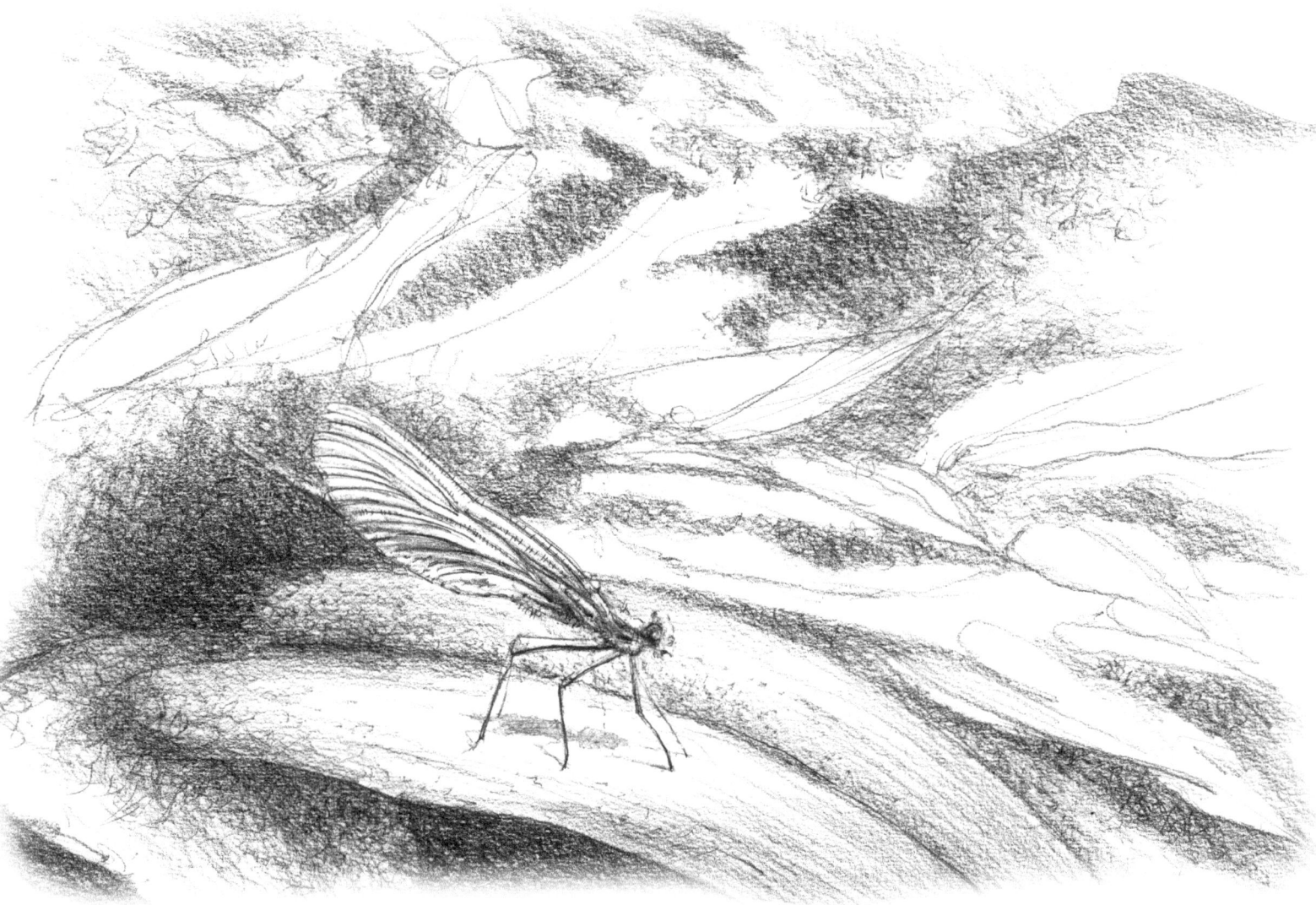

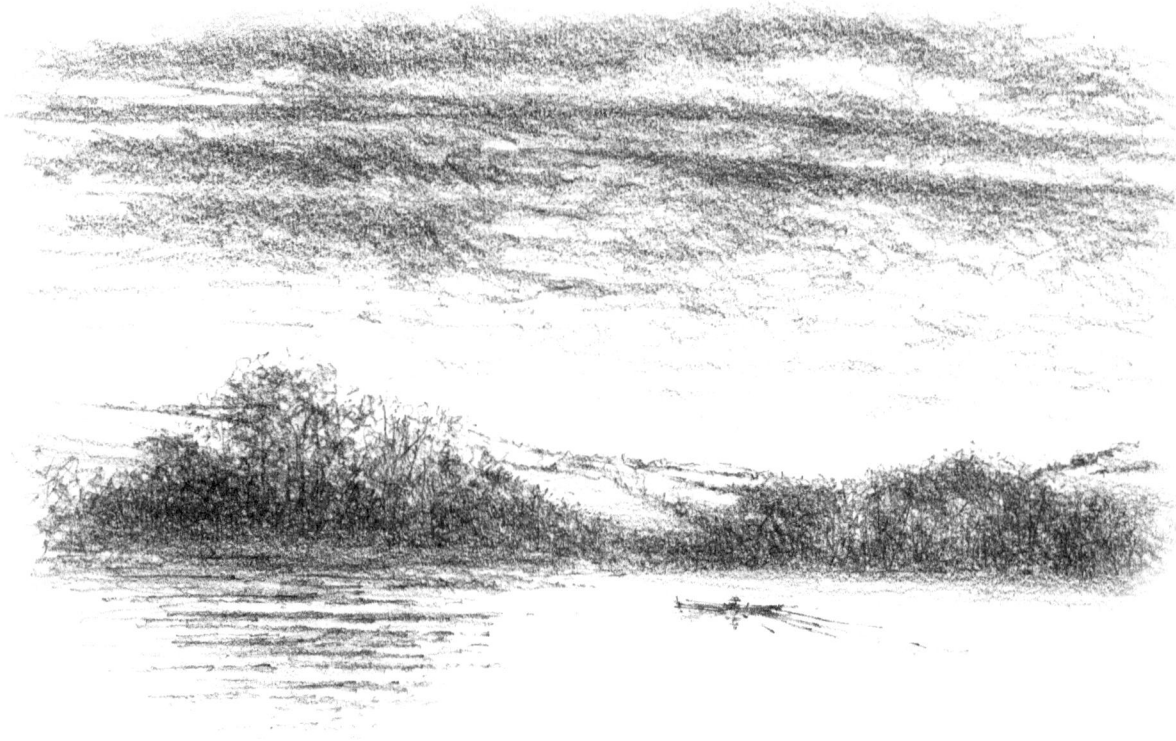

The Poacher
Pencil 290 x 420 mm

The salmon make their way upriver and the poacher casts his net.

MOORLAND
MAGIC

Artwork by Al Cazu (Alan G Williamson)

Cazu

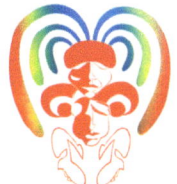

Productions & Publishing

e-mail: mail@alcazu.com

Tel: 07745606275

To view a full catalogue of artwork
by Al Cazu:
www.cazu.co.uk

www.ingramcontent.com/pod-product-compliance
Lightning Source LLC
Chambersburg PA
CBHW050757180526
45159CB00003B/1498